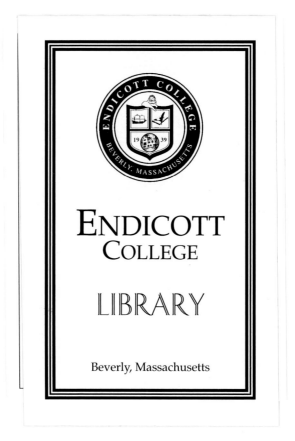

ENDICOTT
COLLEGE

LIBRARY

Beverly, Massachusetts

FUNDAMENTAL APPROACHES
TO
SINGLE SUBJECT DESIGN
AND
ANALYSIS

FUNDAMENTAL APPROACHES
TO
SINGLE SUBJECT DESIGN
AND
ANALYSIS

Curtis H. Krishef
Florida State University

KRIEGER PUBLISHING COMPANY
MALABAR, FLORIDA
1991

Original Edition 1991

Printed and Published by
KRIEGER PUBLISHING COMPANY
KRIEGER DRIVE
MALABAR, FLORIDA 32950

Library of Congress Cataloging-In-Publication Data
Krishef, Curtis H.
    Fundamental approaches to single subject design and analysis/by Curtis H. Krishef.—Original ed.
      p.   cm.
    Includes index.
      ISBN 0-89464-520-X (acid free paper)
      1. Single subject research. I. Title.
BF76.6.S56K75 1991
300′.72—dc20
                                                    90-5328
                                                      CIP

10 9 8 7 6 5 4 3 2

To Ashley and Kyle Norris

CONTENTS

viii   Contents

PREFACE

This book was written for one major purpose: to offer an understandable source of information for both students and practitioners about the study of single subjects. Upon completion of the book the reader should be able to read and interpret the literature concerned with single subject research. I hope this book will also provide those who read it with sufficient knowledge to be able to design studies and analyze data.

Every effort has been made to explain each concept as clearly as possible and to write in language that is easy to understand. During more than 25 years of teaching research and statistics I have found that most students and practitioners are happy to eschew these types of courses. Some try to circumvent research and statistics courses at any cost and when the courses are part of the required curriculum they often enter the classroom with glazed eyes and trepidation. It is generally accepted on most campuses that research and statistics courses are the least liked and are considered to have the least relevance for careers in the helping professions.

This is an unfortunate state of affairs because many students tend to complete their degree requirements with minimal research skills and thus seldom engage in research in their own chosen career fields. The stock answer that I have often heard from the uninterested or the fearful is "I'll let someone else do it." Or "I'll hire a consultant."

Yet today there is an increasing need for professional workers to be familiar with and to do quality research. It is imperative that practitioners working with clients should be interested in determining whether their interventions can be improved, should be dropped, might be altered, or perhaps be continued. This book should ease the task of trying to ferret out an understandable single subject methodology. There are also step by step procedures describing various forms of data analysis that can be used to evaluate treatment and client progress.

This book has been written for all students in the behavioral sciences as well as for the professional teacher or clinical practitioner who wants to know whether a particular intervention has been (1) of no consequence, (2) helpful or, (3) perhaps even harmful. Without studying what is useful treatment and what is not, those professional workers who are trying to help others will certainly be restricted to a very limited understanding about the effectiveness of their efforts. In addition, contributions to the professional literature reach a point of diminishing returns if articles from workers are purely exhortative or contain little or no research documentation.

I have not covered the more complex designs or involved forms of data analysis. Many of these, sometimes because of the number of data points required, are difficult to implement in clinical settings. Some methods, such as the Autoregressive Integrated Moving Averages approach, call for the researcher to build empirical models based upon rather extended studies with anywhere from 50 to 100 observations. The magnitude of data requirements are both extensive and complex and more often than not necessitate the use of a computer, thus going beyond the scope of this book.

Research methodology on single subjects is a rapidly evolving area. There are many differences of opinion by extremely knowledgeable researchers that remain unresolved. Certain forms of statistical analysis are held by some to be most appropriate for single subject research and by others to be totally inappropriate. Some researchers tout charting techniques and feel that statistics are unnecessary for analyzing data on single subjects. Others feel just the opposite and believe that graphs or charts also present problems of interpretation. I belong to the group that believes graphing and statistics should be considered as complementary methods and each should be selectively used for the most effective analysis and interpretation of data.

Not only is there controversy among single subject researchers about the use of statistics or graphing for interpreting data, there are differences of opinions among proponents of single subject and group comparison research designs. Single subject research designs are usually viewed as quasi-experimental by those who support the group type approach and are, therefore, considered less precise and less accurate than the true experimental designs. It is true that single subject research is still in its beginning evolutionary stages, but time will certainly bring forth contributors who will increase the level of sophistication and knowledge about single subject research.

It seems there is ample room for both single and group approaches to understanding human behavior. Single subject research is needed to answer questions about the effects of specific treatments on individuals over time. Information from single subject studies helps to document how individuals change. With single subject methodology there is no need to compromise the effects of treatment on different subjects by averaging data across groups as is done with group comparison designs. On the other hand, single subject designs do have limitations. For example, it is very difficult to generalize findings, even to a group of similar subjects, based upon information obtained from a single individual. Alternately, group designs are very useful when questions exist about shared characteristics of groups or when a research-practitioner wishes to generalize treatment effects across groups of subjects.

Writing this book has been a labor of both love and tediousness. I sincerely hope that the results of this effort will be helpful to those who wish to engage in, or better understand the methodology of single subject research.

CHAPTER 1

INTRODUCTION TO THE USE OF SINGLE SUBJECT RESEARCH

Research methodology that studies a single individual, object, or event, has been variously known as: single case, case-study, same-subject, intra-subject, repeated measures, intensive, clinical-experimental, applied behavior analysis, single subject, time series, single system, ideographic, and N = 1, research. Throughout the balance of this book only the terms single case or single subject will be the primary terminology that will be used to reduce confusion and keep the language as simple and straightforward as possible.

Single subject designs differ from the group designs in three ways: (1) only a single person is studied rather than a group of people, (2) the results of the study are based upon the repeated collection of information about one individual, and (3) at some time during the evaluation the individual is given a treatment. The term *treatment* generally refers to the independent variable's effect or impact on the dependent variable.

There are those who advocate the single case type of research as the best approach for use by a practitioner (Briar, 1978). Thomas (1975) said that the single case method provides the clinician with a unique opportunity to integrate research techniques into clinical practice. Those who believe in the merits of the single case method feel that it permits the practitioner to validate empirically a treatment modality without having to use the traditional group-type comparison procedure. Group procedures are often difficult for the practitioner to implement in a clinical setting. The application of a single case approach in clinical psychology (Leitenberg, 1973), psychiatry (Barlow and Hersen, 1973), education (Risley and Wolfe, 1972; Thoresen, 1972), social work practice, (Thomas, 1978), physical rehabilitation, (Martin and Epstein, 1976), and behavioral medicine (Barlow, Blanchard, Hayes, and Epstein, 1977), attests to the rather widespread popularity of the single subject methodology. This method of study can provide for empirical testing of one type of treatment as well as the development of treatment packages that contain more than one intervention technique.

HISTORICAL OVERVIEW

The first use of single subject designs has generally been dated to the 1830s beginning with the physiological studies of Johannes Mueller and Laude Bernard (Barlow and Hersen, 1984). Some 30 years later the approach was again described by Fechner in his 1860 publication *Elemente der Psychophysik*, often considered as a beginning text in the field of experimental psychology (Hersen, 1982). Fechner described studies he had done with single subjects to determine sensory thresholds. Subsequent to Fechner's studies in psychophysics, Wundt using a single subject design, studied sensation and perception as did Ebbinghaus (1885) who investigated memory.

Ebbinghaus's skillfully conducted work established the foundation for much of the research on verbal learning that was carried out during the past century (McGeoch and Irion, 1952). His main findings, drawn from self-administered learning situations involving about 2,000 lists of nonsense syllables and 42 stanzas of poetry, are studied today by those interested in understanding the construct of memory. Another early single subject study contributing to learning theory, was that of Bryan and Harter (1899) who used a "letter-word-phrase" analysis of learning enabling them to arrive at an understanding of learning plateaus. Their findings were based upon observations of only one student.

Most students of perception are familiar with the work of Stratton (1897) who studied the confusion caused by using inverted eye lenses. For his research Stratton himself served as his own single subject (Boring, 1942). Another single subject design that many psychology students are familiar with is the work of Kellogg and Kellogg (1933) with a young chimpanzee named Gus. By using a single chimpanzee subject the Kelloggs tried to determine whether early experiences modified behaviors that were traditionally regarded as instinctive.

Physiologists Cannon and Washburn (1912), using recordings of Washburn's peristaltic responses, documented that whenever Washburn felt hunger pangs there were associated stomach constrictions.

In a classical research effort Watson and Rayner (1920) studied Albert, a little boy who was conditioned to fear a white rat. Each time Albert would reach for the animal a loud noise was made which frightened the child. The Watson-Raynor effort was terminated before the fear removal part of the experiment could be completed because Albert moved away. Jones (1924), however, using a child named Peter, was able to show that reconditioning could overcome a non-laboratory produced fear of white furry objects.

Prince (1905) performed an impressive piece of research on a single subject when he brought the attention of professionals to Miss Beauchamp who for many years served as the model case representing multiple personality problems. Shipley (1961) described the single subject research efforts of Wundt and Pavlov among others in his book covering 36 research studies. All of these early researchers used single case analysis as their method for analyzing data.

From 1925 until 1963 a total of 246 single subject studies appeared in professional journals (Dukes, 1965) and although these 246 studies represented a relatively small percentage of the total of all studies during those years, single subject research was found in sufficient quantity to indicate that it had been a fairly well established method of investigation.

After World War II, a serious reemergence of single case studies occurred. This was particularly evident in the works of B. F. Skinner. Skinner (1966) clearly explained his philosophy of research when he wrote "instead of studying a thousand rats for one hour each, or a hundred rats for ten hours each, the investigator is likely to study one rat for a thousand hours" (p. 21).

In 1960 Sidman published *Tactics of Scientific Research*. It was a compilation of specific experimental strategies that could be used in the analysis of animal behavior. This publication was followed for the next three decades by several other behavior therapy publications which summarized the study of human behavior using the single case methodology.

THE IMPACT OF THE GROUP COMPARISON DESIGNS

During the 1930s an increased use of the group comparison approach began. The development of inferential statistics, although advanced by many people, was in large measure founded on the efforts and genius of two major contributors. The first was Sir Ronald Fisher. Fisher

(1890–1962) coined the term "null hypothesis" and published numerous papers in the areas of experimental design, randomization to eliminate bias, statistics, and statistical genetics. He also developed the "analysis of variance" procedure in statistics.

The second individual who made enormous contributions to the field of group statistics was Karl Pearson (1857–1936). Pearson has at times been referred to as the founder of statistics. He coined the term "standard deviation" and was basically responsible for the theory underlying correlation analysis. He made significant contributions to the field of probability distributions and created the chi-square nonparametric statistic. During the late 1940s and 1950s, several large-scale group comparison studies were undertaken to determine the effects of various therapeutic approaches. Eysenck (1952) evaluated the improvement rate of clients treated by psychotherapy and compared them with the spontaneous remission rates of untreated subjects using insurance records. He found that the benefits to individuals based on psychotherapeutic treatment were essentially nonexistent. A few years later Bergin (1966) obtained different findings when his studies revealed that some individuals improved as a result of psychotherapy, and some actually got worse. Bergin felt that using traditional group type statistics produced an averaging effect which created negligible results and that these forms of statistics had probably cancelled out the positive treatment results of many patients who had been studied.

The Bergin study (1966) was one of the first to produce results questioning the findings of group comparison statistics that had been used for studying outcomes of psychotherapeutic treatments. The validity of the results obtained by group type statistical comparisons became dubious, because while these forms of statistics were considered highly accurate, they also had some inherent deficiencies possibly leading to misinterpretation of results. These deficiencies have been well summarized by many researchers (Hersen and Barlow, 1976; Kratochwill, Mott, and Dodson, 1984; Rabin, 1981; Strupp and Bergin, 1969; Johnson and Pennypacker, 1980; Levy, 1983). The limitations of group types of analyses noted by Hersen and Barlow (1976) included: (1) ethical objections by practitioners to the waiting list or placebo control group; (2) practical problems in developing homogeneous client groups; (3) financial cost of the group comparison approach; (4) obscuring of individual outcomes in the group average; (5) difficulty in generalizing group comparison results to individual clients; and (6) the frequent use of the pretest and posttest research design method. The pretest-posttest design results can be difficult to interpret because of certain threats to internal validity such as unknown changes that may occur between the pretest and the posttest periods.

Bergin and Strupp (1970) believed that the use of group comparison designs, and the statistical analysis connected with such designs, restricted the development of psychotherapeutic research. They noted that, when individuals were averaged, many of the outcome studies provided equivocal results. The averaging tended to decrease discrimination between individuals and limit determination as to why certain individuals progressed with treatment while others either remained the same or deteriorated.

THE CURRENT CONTROVERSY ABOUT THE BEST METHOD TO ANALYZE DATA OBTAINED FROM SINGLE SUBJECT RESEARCH

For many years most researchers using single subject studies graphed the data that they gathered and made visual inspections of their graphs to see whether important changes in targeted behaviors had occurred between baseline and treatment observations. (Parsonson and Baer, 1978; Sidman, 1960). There were those, however, who criticized the visual method of assessing data because they felt that it was not sufficiently sensitive or reliable (DeProspero and Cohen, 1979; Furlong and Wampold, 1981; Jones, Weinrott, and Vaught, 1978). Some suggested that certain forms of statistical analysis could be used in place of graphed data (Kazdin, 1976; Kratochwill, 1978; Shine and Bower, 1971). The problem was that traditional group types of statistical analyses were generally inappropriate for single subject data (Scheffe, 1959; Toothaker, Banz, Noble, Camp, and Davis, 1983). The primary difficulty with traditional statistics is their intolerance to data which is serially dependent. Serial dependence, also known as autocorrelation, means that each successive observation in a given study provides information which allows one to predict subsequent behavior based on previous behavior. Most single subject studies tend to provide statistically dependent data because the previous observations of a person's behavior are predictive of that individual's future behavior.

Several authors have suggested different ways of overcoming the inadequacies of traditional group types of statistics. Time series analysis, as suggested by Box and Jenkins (1970), is one form of statistical procedure that has been proposed for use with traditional group types of statistics because the procedure itself transforms serially dependent data. The operation, however, is not a simple methodology to use. Besides requiring considerable statistical expertise it usually requires computer analysis.

Other writers have suggested that instead of using the normal distribution probabilities associated with such statistics as the t test or ANOVA, which are ordinarily based upon independent data, probabilities should be computed against the original data of a study and the statistic, whether a t test or ANOVA, should then be recomputed to determine whether the result would show a statistically significant change.

Still others have proposed binomial tests such as the split-middle or celeration line techniques to study changes in trend between phases of a study. Some have said that it makes no difference whether the data are serially related when the binomial test is used. Critics, with opposing views, maintain that the use of autocorrelated data is inappropriate with binomial tests because such data violate the assumptions upon which the binomial is based.

It is recognized at the outset that statistical analysis of single subject data, only evaluates whether a change is found that is statistically significant. No validation is made about the reasons for the change in behavior, only that it occurred. Also, when behavioral change has been found to be statistically significant such results may or may not necessarily have meaning in practice. Even modest behavioral changes, in some instances, might be much more important to the practitioner than finding statistical significance.

Statistical analysis has one advantage in that it provides the research-practitioner with a relatively reliable standard for drawing conclusions about study data. Correctly used, statistics can tell the researcher whether a specific treatment or intervention has resulted in fairly small, but consistent effects. If, in fact, statistical analyses provide information about such small effects it might be possible to manipulate and arrange various forms of the treatment to produce even greater desired change. Additionally, much remains unknown about human behavior, and because of this paucity, statistics can be useful for comparing a wide range of intervention techniques which might not be readily analyzable by graphing methods.

The entire field of data analysis concerned with single subject research is still highly controversial. There are critics and proponents for different procedures who argue vehemently among themselves. It is the contention of this author that statistical analysis is a method for complementing visual analysis and statistics can be used to strengthen the conclusions that are drawn from plotting and visually inspecting data. Despite differences of opinion about the use of statistics as well as some inadequacies in the statistical procedures that will be outlined in this book, statistics do provide an acceptable means for assessing change in client behavior. This book focuses on both graphing and statistics because both are important methods for interpreting data. Each of these methods serves to facilitate the expansion of knowledge about intervention techniques with individual clients. Clinicians, therefore, should familiarize themselves with some of the more fundamental statistical as well as graphing procedures that are applicable to single subject research.

CHAPTER 2

THE TIME SERIES APPROACH

The term "time series research" generally connotes the measurement of an individual (or a group) over time intervals. The purpose is to determine the effect of a selected type of treatment or intervention on a particular behavior. Under the general rubric of "time series research" there are the "time series designs" and "time series analysis." "Time series designs" represent a wide variety of research methods, applicable to both individuals and/or groups, that use the concept of time as a primary variable. Once a "time series design" has been established and data have been collected "time series analysis" is concerned with the statistical evaluation of the data that has been obtained. Certain forms of time series analysis become quite involved and may require the use of computer programs. There are several models available, each with different formulas and assumptions. Because of the complications involved with certain types of "time series analysis," these will not be covered in this book.*

Some readers may be familiar with, or perhaps may have heard of, "repeated measures designs" that are applied to large group factorial experiments. Repeated measures designs are not to be confused with time series designs. Repeated measures use replicated observation of a specified treatment which is considered to be a random factor. The random factor is then crossed with a fixed factor and the crossing of a replication (random factor) with a fixed factor is referred to as a *block*. The repeated measurement of a series of blocks is called a *repeated measures design*. The repeated measures design is in no way similar to the time series design which observes and measures the treatment effect on a single unit of analysis over phases of time.

*For an excellent discussion on Time Series Analysis see Thomas R. Kratochwill's book *Single Subject Research–Strategies for Evaluating Change*, Academic Press, New York, 1978.

TIME SERIES DESIGNS AND BASIC PROCEDURES

The coverage of material on basic procedures related to time series designs, although brief, should be sufficient to provide the reader with an adequate introduction to this subject. Information about these designs will supply both a knowledge base as well as an awareness of the appropriate procedures to be used.

Probably the most outstanding feature of the single case approach is the repeated measurement of a single subject under controlled conditions. The repetition is performed to establish a cause-and-effect relationship between the independent and dependent variables (Kratochwill, 1978). To assess this relationship a research-practitioner should be alert to the following: (1) make a conscious effort to identify and clearly define the independent and dependent variables, (2) develop a procedure for the measurement of these variables, (3) decide upon the research design that is most appropriate for the study, taking into consideration the maximum degree of experimental control, (4) secure a suitable baseline of data; (5) determine the lengths of the various baseline and treatment phases in which one, and only one, independent variable can be manipulated at a time, (6) be cognizant of the problems that **irreversible** procedures may create. Behaviors that cannot be reversed are called irreversible. For example, once a child has improved in reading level, the child's reading cannot be reversed to its original point, (7) be familiar with methods for analyzing data and (8) try, when possible, to replicate results.

Collecting Data on a Single Subject

Before collecting any data for the study of a single person, single group, single organization, or any other single unit of analysis, the first step is to define the characteristics of the behavior that is to be assessed. Sometimes the behavior is relatively easy to define and record but at other times may almost defy definition, or may be exceedingly difficult to record. Simple behavior easily defined and recorded might be: walking, crawling, absences from school, thumb sucking, reading at a specific grade level, or time spent in bed. More complex behaviors might be: aberrant sexual thoughts, feelings of depression and euphoria, or negative self-concept.

METHODS OF OBSERVATION

Once the researcher has operationalized a definition for the behavior to be studied, then a method for observing the behavior must be established. There are essentially three methods for observing behavior.

The first is to record how frequently a single behavior occurs within a specified time frame. For example, a researcher might want to know the number of temper tantrums displayed by a young child during an eight-hour day.

A second method of observation is to record how long a particular behavior occurs. For example, by timing, a researcher could determine how long each temper tantrum lasted.

A third procedure involves recording whether or not a targeted behavior occurs during a specified time frame. For example, starting when the child awoke each day, and at 15-minute intervals, a record could be kept showing whether the child did or did not have a temper tantrum in each 15-minute interval.

Accurately recording observations is very important if the research effort is to produce correct results. As stated previously the behaviors must be clearly defined, but in addition there must be a description of the type of setting where the research will take place, clarity about the methods that will be used to gather data, and special care to train observers to assure agreement about the behaviors being studied. To determine the extent of agreement, if there is more than one observer, researchers often use specific time periods when the observers are asked to record the occurrence of the behavior(s) under study. The degree of agreement, or reliability, is then reported either as a percentage of agreement between observers or as a correlation coefficient. Depending upon the nature of the research, Hersen and Barlow (1976) recommend an 80% agreement between observers as minimally acceptable, while Gingerich (1979) recommends at least 90% ratio of agreements to total observations.

THREATS TO INTERNAL VALIDITY
IN SINGLE CASE DESIGNS

The effect of a particular intervention or treatment using group type designs is often interpreted by comparing pretest data with posttest data or by comparing an experimental (treatment) group with a control (non-treatment) group. The effectiveness of treatment in single case designs is usually based upon the comparison of measurements of the dependent variable between phases. The design selected for a single subject study can have a significant affect upon the ability of the researcher to make interpretations.

If the design does not control for extraneous variables, valid conclusions cannot be drawn and the design is said to lack internal validity. Jayaratne (1978) proposed that the strength of the internal validity of a design is based upon the question "Did the treatment cause the change in the behavior, or is there another plausible explanation?" (p. 38). If explanations other than the treatment can be given for the change in the dependent (outcome) variable, the design has low internal validity (Cook and Campbell, 1979).

Kratochwill (1978) presented a thorough discussion of validity threats in single subject research. He noted that most of the sources of invalidity listed by Campbell and Stanley (1963) for group comparisons are also found in single subject designs. The following are major types of rival hypotheses (threats to internal validity) which call into question any possibility that the researcher can make an assumption that the treatment or intervention actually produced the outcome. The following sources of internal invalidity are common to both group and single subject designs:

1. History—pertains to those environmental events that occur during a study that are potential influences on the subject. When studying people no one can isolate those who are being studied from environment(s) that may affect the research that is being conducted. To compensate for this confounding factor, group studies use what are called a control or nontreatment group. In single subject studies the individual serves as his or her own control through the use of a baseline.

2. Maturation—refers to those results that can occur just because a client (subject) continues to grow and change in keeping with normal human development. Any findings in a study that occur because of maturational change, rather than as a result of the treatment, are considered to be threats to internal validity creating rival answers and spurious conclusions.

3. Testing—is concerned with those conditions resulting from the use of a measurement tool which in turn affects the behavior of a subject.

For example, a pretest could give a subject experiences and knowledge which in turn might help that individual to improve his or her performance on a posttest. The improvement could not be attributed to benefits derived from the treatment but only to having learned something while taking a pretest which later helped to improve the posttest scores.

4. Instrumentation—refers to any influences that might occur which will alter research results because of changes in the measuring instrument or changes in observers, raters or interviewers. For example, observers become more skilled in their roles as they continue to serve as observers and they may be more accurate as they gain experience. On the other hand observers might fatigue after a time and their accuracy would then diminish.

5. Experimental mortality—refers to the client who drops out over the course of a study. The person who drops out may be quite different from one who remains with the study, thus leading to the possibility of invalid conclusions. This threat is also sometimes referred to as "attrition."

6. Statistical regression—is the tendency for extreme scores on any measure to regress toward the mean of a distribution when the measurement device is given again. Any individual selected for a study whose score on the dependent variable is extreme, such as very high or very low test scores, will tend to obtain scores on subsequent tests that are closer to the population mean. A single subject example would be the selection of a child with an extremely high score on a mathematics test who, if given a second administration of a similar mathematics test, would tend to have a lower score. Or, taking an example from a group type design, if a group of children with extremely low scores were selected for study, they would have a tendency on subsequent testing to have higher scores. It can be predicted that any group of individuals selected for study who have very high or very low scores will statistically move (regress) toward the mean of the group. If they start with very high scores they will regress downward toward the population mean and if they start with very low scores they will regress upward toward the population mean.

7. Multiple intervention interference—occurs when two or more treatments are introduced in succession. This poses a threat to internal validity because the treatments may well interfere with themselves.

The effect of the later treatments are difficult to evaluate because of the manner in which the client may have been affected by earlier treatments.

8. Instability—happens because of natural variations in the data which may result in spurious findings depending upon the degree of variability that can be found in the data. Generally, the more the variability the less reliable the results.

9. Interactions—a potential rival explanation of results which can take place when any combination of the above threats occur together. For example, any person who is getting better as time goes on (maturation) may be more likely to drop out (mortality).

Being aware of the limitation of each type of single case design is important in order to recognize the threats to internal validity that have just been reviewed.

A BRIEF OVERVIEW OF SINGLE CASE DESIGNS

The basic model of a true single case design is usually referred to as the A-B-A design. This design has a number of different variations ranging from the simplest, the A-B design, to more complex interaction designs such as A-B-A-B-BC. Because there are so many forms, many of which are quite difficult to apply in clinical settings, only the more fundamental single case designs will be covered. These basic designs are useful to nearly all practitioners although as a general rule the more fundamental the design the less control there will be over threats to internal validity.

One form of single subject design is called the "case study." The case study may have either (1) the A phase—observation of a subject or, (2) the B phase—treatment while observing the subject. These designs use only one time phase of either observation alone (A) or treatment with observation (B).

Case Study Designs

A case study consists of professional observation of an individual client. Although relatively easy to perform, case studies are also very limited in what they tell a researcher. This deficiency results from failure to control for most threats to internal validity. Case study designs, however, can be valuable because they may provide some support to suggest that a particular practice technique is working. Additionally, case studies may provide useful preliminary information for a more controlled study. Because of their inherent limitations, the results of case studies should be interpreted with caution.

The two most common forms of case studies are the **observation only** and **treatment** (or intervention) **only** designs. The first, "observation only," is shown in Figure 2-1.

Figure 2-1 depicts O_1, O_2, O_3 and O_n as a series of observations that have been made within an A time frame without any follow-up intervention or treatment.

The second type of case study design is concerned only with a treatment and is shown in Figure 2-2.

The Treatment Only Design uses XO_1 to illustrate the first treatment and accompaning observation applied during the treatment or B phase, XO_2 the second, XO_3 the third, and XO_n the last treatment and observation. There are no phase "A" or baseline observations.

The "A" or "B" only case study approaches are essentially practitioner types of designs that can be used to secure a better understanding of client behavior without necessarily trying to draw any reliable conclusions from the results.

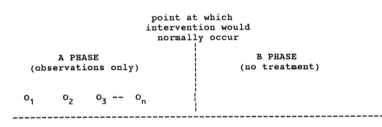

```
                        point at which
                     intervention would
                       normally occur
                              |
        A PHASE               |        B PHASE
    (observations only)       |      (no treatment)
                              |
                              |
     O₁     O₂    O₃ -- Oₙ    |
                              |
---------------------------------------------------------------
```

Figure 2-1 Observation only design without treatment

```
        Point at which intervention would normally occur
              if there were baseline observations
                              |
        A PHASE               |        B PHASE
                              |
    without observation       |      treatment only
                              |
                              |       XO₁    XO₂    XO₃ -- XOₙ
                              |
```

Figure 2-2 Treatment only design without prior observation

The A-B Design

The A-B design is the most basic form of the single subject designs. It has two time frames. The first frame, called the "A" phase, is the **baseline** or the pretreatment period in which information is collected before a treatment is given to the client. During the "A" phase, or "baseline period," a client's behavior is observed for a sufficient length of time to determine the frequency of the behavioral pattern that is being studied. Once there is a fairly stable occurrence of the behavior, the "baseline" or "A" phase is terminated and a "B" phase is begun. The time represented by the "B" phase is the **treatment** (or intervention) period of the research. During the "B" time frame the experimental variable, for example counseling of a client, is initiated. There must also be a sufficient period of time devoted to the treatment or "B" phase to ascertain what the effects of the treatment might be. Letters typically used to depict single subject designs adhere to the general rule that the letter "A" represents baseline data and all other letters such as "B," "C," "D," etc., represent different treatments. If the baseline period shown as "A" is followed by a "B" it means there was only one baseline which came first and one treatment or independent variable that followed. If the design is shown as B-A-B it means that treatment "B" was given first; followed by a "no treatment" period shown as "A," which was then followed by the same treatment "B" as was given in the beginning.

Returning to the A-B design it is depicted as seen in Figure 2-3.

In Figure 2-3 the baseline period, or phase "A," consists of O_1 representing the first baseline observation, O_2 the second baseline observation, O_3 the third baseline observation, and O_7 the last baseline observation needed to establish a relatively stable trend. The X represents the point at which a treatment or intervention is begun; and XO_8

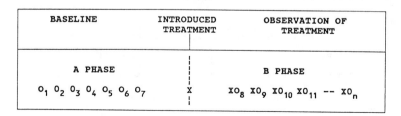

Figure 2-3 The A-B design

represents the first observation during the treatment or "B" phase, XO_9 the second observation during treatment (or ninth of the total number of observations), XO_{10} the third treatment observation, and XO_n the last observation considered necessary to establish the effect, if any, of the treatment.

Example of an A-B Design

As an example, an A-B design might be used to determine the effect of a child counseling program for reducing the incidence of acting-out problems. A graph using this design is plotted in Figure 2-4.

Observation and the A-B Design

The frequency of behavior problems shown in Figure 2-4 were observed during baseline period "A." A behavior modification program, using praise as a reinforcer, was then introduced as the treatment or "B" phase during which time the child was also observed. Notice that the frequency of displayed difficulties rise during the baseline. After the intervention the frequency of behavior problems tends to decline.

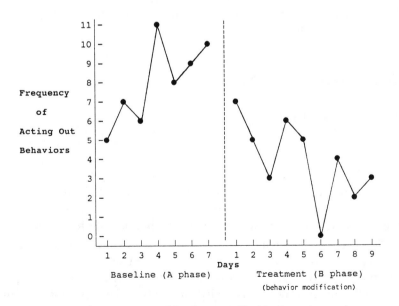

Figure 2-4 The frequency of acting out behaviors in a six-year old child over 7 baseline and 9 treatment days.

Advantages and Disadvantages of the A-B Design

The A-B design improves upon the inadequacies of the "observation only" or "treatment only" case study designs. This design permits a practitioner to compare the behavior of a client both before and during a treatment. The A-B design is quite common in clinical settings because it is fairly easy for practitioners to carry out. A disadvantage of the A-B design is it's failure to control for most of the threats to internal validity, such as history, maturation, testing, or instrumentation.

The example in Figure 2-4 shows that the undesirable behaviors were rising during baseline and declined after the treatment or intervention was begun. The decline, however, may not be attributable to the treatment but rather to history. Something may have occurred in the child's life coincidentally with the time when the treatment was begun that produced the downward shift in negative behaviors. The clinical researcher does not know for sure whether it was the treatment or one of the uncontrolled threats to internal validity that produced the downward direction of undesirable behaviors. Because the A-B design does not control for rival answers to the results obtained, does not make this design useless. On the contrary the A-B design can be very helpful to the practitioner-researcher in assessing whether, and how much, the behavior under consideration has changed even though such change may not be unequivocally assigned to the treatment.

WITHDRAWAL DESIGNS

The A-B-A Design

One extension of the A-B design is the A-B-A design which includes an additional series of baseline observations after treatment. The format for this design is shown in Figure 2-5.

The major characteristic of the A-B-A design is that it involves a **reversal** or **withdrawal** of treatment in an attempt to return to the conditions that existed during the first baseline period. Reversal of the treatment variable typically means that the treatment during the B phase, is withdrawn. Leitenberg (1973), however, has suggested a more definitive distinction between reversal and withdrawal designs. He proposed that a reversal design is really an inappropriate title for a design where treatment is simply withdrawn. According to Leitenberg a re-

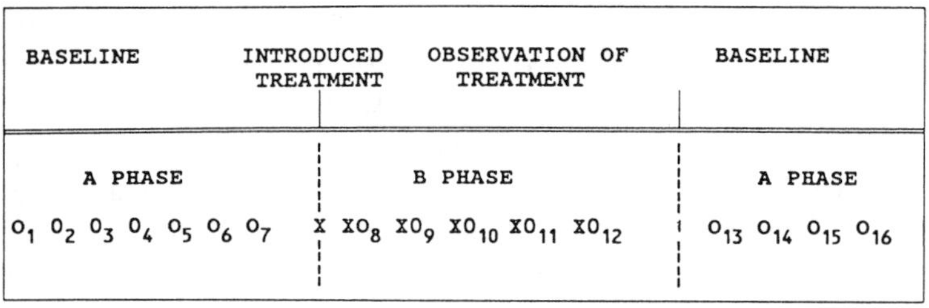

BASELINE	INTRODUCED TREATMENT	OBSERVATION OF TREATMENT	BASELINE
A PHASE		B PHASE	A PHASE
O_1 O_2 O_3 O_4 O_5 O_6 O_7	X	XO_8 XO_9 XO_{10} XO_{11} XO_{12}	O_{13} O_{14} O_{15} O_{16}

Figure 2-5 The A-B-A single subject design

versal design would not be the mere withdrawal of treatment but rather an attempt to reverse the behavior to its original state after the treatment.

With the A-B-A design the clinician establishes a baseline, initiates treatment, and then withdraws (or perhaps attempts to reverse) the treatment to see if the targeted behavior returns to the baseline condition. The question might well be asked, "if the treatment seems to be working why withdraw its benefits and return to a baseline?" The answer is, if the first baseline behavior (Phase A) changed as a result of a treatment (Phase B), and after withdrawing the treatment the behavior returned to its approximate original baseline level (Phase A), then the treatment certainly would appear to have had an effect on the client's behavior. Without withdrawal of the treatment the worker would not be as assured that the intervention had actually produced an effect on the client's behavior. Lacking this confirmation, serious question could be raised about whether something additional to the treatment could have been taking place that changed the client's behavior.

Advantages and Disadvantages of the A-B-A Design

This design still does not control for many of the threats to internal validity. As is the case for some other types of single subject designs, the A-B-A design can control for mortality because only one subject is used. Also by definition, selection, which is a systematic bias in selecting subjects, should not be a problem with the A-B-A design. Maturation, instrumentation and regression might all pose problems with the A-B-A design, but most likely the major threat to internal validity comes from history. Various conditions occurring during the study of a single subject can have considerable impact on the person's behavior, exclusive of the treatments that are being administered. The A-B-A design offers greater opportunity for inferring causality than the A-B designs because the practitioner now has three phases instead of two from which to draw conclusions.

While withdrawal of treatment to see if the client's behavior returns to baseline level may be a good way of determining whether the treatment has worked, not all situations lend themselves to the use of this design. As mentioned previously certain conditions cannot, or should not, be returned to a baseline level. An example given earlier of treatment that would help a child to improve reading skills more than likely would result in a higher reading level which cannot be changed to its earlier level. Such a condition is considered to be *irreversible* and is inapplicable for use with a withdrawal or reversal type of design. Another condition which is not recommended for this type of design is a treatment which improves social skills. Once the skills are learned they, like reading level, are basically irreversible. There are also times when a client's problem behavior is so severe that it would be inappropriate to withdraw treatment and possibly allow the client to return to unacceptable problem behavior.

Another difficulty with the withdrawal types of designs is the possibility that they may result in wrongful treatment of a client. A counselor must face the dilemma whether it is ethically right to withdraw treatment from a client who seems to be making progress because of that treatment. If what appears to be beneficial treatment of the client is withdrawn this could be interpreted as unethical.

The B-A-B Design

The B-A-B design, another three phase design, has an advantage over the A-B-A design in that the last stage of the design maintains a treatment and does not leave the client with the adverse possibility of ending in a "no treatment" condition. The disadvantage of this type of design is the lack of initial information about the baseline behavior of the individual who is being studied.

The B-C-B Design

This type of single subject design has no "true" baseline period. It begins a research treatment on a client as "B" then changes the treatment to a second procedure as "C" to determine whether even greater improvement can be made and then reverses or withdraws the second treatment, returning to the first treatment phase, which was ''B.'' While the beginning phase ''B'' does not constitute a ''true'' baseline period it might be considered as a modified form of baseline because another treatment ''C'' follows the first treatment phase ''B.''

The A-B-A-B Design

This design, sometimes referred to as the ''equivalent time-samples design,'' has an advantage over the three phase A-B-A design in that it allows the practitioner to withdraw treatment to see if the client's behavior returns to near baseline level. The A-B-A-B design does not leave the client in a ''no treatment'' phase at the end of the research as is the case with the A-B-A design. Another advantage of this design, is that the clinician can watch to see if there has been consistency in the client's change of behavior from the first treatment following baseline to the second treatment following a withdrawal. The A-B-A-B design allows for the repetition of two baselines and two treatments within a single study on one subject. The accuracy of the results are, therefore, considerably strengthened and provide for a much higher degree of reliability concerning the findings than any of the previously described three phase designs.

Variations of the A-B-A-B Design

There are a number of variations which can be used that are basically extensions of the A-B-A-B design. For example, the A-B-A-C-A successive intervention design assesses the impact of two different treatments, treatments B and C, on the dependent variable. However, it does not allow for comparison of the effects of treatments B and C, because of the confounding variable of time (Barlow and Hersen, 1984). There is also an A-B-A-B-A-B continuous intervention design which is also an extended replication of the basic A-B pattern and provides for the development of additional information about the controlling effects of the treatment intervention. Sometimes shorter, fewer phased designs, do not allow the clinician-researcher sufficient time to complete treatment and then the extended designs can be beneficially used. Mann (1972), for example, used the A-B-A-B-A-B extended design when treating overweight subjects because of the time necessary to complete the research.

ADDITIONAL DESIGNS

There are two additional variations of single case designs. The first permits a researcher to either compare two or more interventions across time (between phases), which is called the Alternating Treatment Design. The second allows the researcher to compare effects of increasing intensity of an intervention, called the Changing Intensity Design.

Alternating Treatment Designs

The Alternating Treatment Design has essentially four phases. The first consists of a baseline observation period. The second, the alternating use of two different treatments or interventions. Third, the review and appraisal as to which treatment appeared to be more effective. Fourth, the continued use of the more effective treatment if further change in behavior is desired.

Over time several different names have been given to this type of design. Various authors have called it, "multiple schedule design," "multi-element baseline," "randomization design," and "simultaneous treatment design." The "alternating treatment design" first named by Barlow and Hayes (1979), allows a researcher to compare the effects of two or more treatments on a single subject (Kazdin and Geesey, 1977; Kazdin and Hartmann, 1978).

Taking an example from a marital relationship, if a research oriented wife wished to increase her husband's verbal interaction with her during evening hours, she might want to determine which of two forms of positive reinforcement, smiling at her husband or touching him after each interaction, was more effective in increasing verbal exchanges. She would initially conduct a baseline phase over several consecutive evenings observing the level of her husband's verbal behavior. Once she had a stable pattern, she would institute her program. She would randomly select, by tossing a coin, which of the two treatments, either smiling or touching, would be used on the first evening. Whichever treatment the coin dictated would be used first. If she decided to use two hour intervals the first treatment would be employed for the first two hours and the second treatment during the next two hours of the first evening. On following nights she would reverse the sequence.

The reversing of the treatment sequence is called a *counterbalancing* procedure where the treatments are given in an inverse order. A purely random selection of the two treatments each evening might not work

Table 2-1 Treatment A "Smiling" and Treatment B "Touching" for Alternating Treatment Design

Evenings

		First	Second	Third	Fourth
H	First	A	B	A	B
O		B	A	B	A
U					
R	Second	B	A	B	A
S		A	B	A	B

well because it is possible that the random selection might produce the same sequencing for several nights in a row. By using a counterbalancing methodology the wife would reduce the effect of one treatment constantly preceding the other and, therefore, perhaps continuously affecting the next treatment.

"Multiple-treatment interference" can result when two treatments are given in relatively quick order. One form of "multiple-treatment interference" occurs when the order of the treatments might influence the results that are obtained. When the order of the treatment interferes with the results it is called "sequential confounding" or "order effects." Also under "multiple-treatment interference" there may be a problem of "carry-over" where one treatment influences the following treatment even though there may be no overall sequential confounding. "Carry-over" is commonly encountered in the daily activities of most people. For example, if one smells a bottle of perfume at a department store counter, the next perfume that is smelled may be considerably affected by the odor from the first. The sense of smell has been compromised and the same thing can happen in research. Counterbalancing, therefore, attempts to avoid both "sequential confounding" as well as "carry-over" effects.

After conducting an equal distribution of the treatment interventions for a reasonable period, (at least two evenings) the wife would then compare the frequency of her husband's verbal interactions with her that were associated with each reinforcer. This would indicate which of the two reinforcers was more effective. She might then want to continue to use the more effective reinforcer if she wanted to increase her husband's verbal interactions. Table 2-1 shows the alternating treatments for the above design.

Advantages and Disadvantages of the Alternating Treatment Design

This design can be used only with two baseline observations and a minimum of two different administrations of treatments. Thus, extended observations are not possible with an "alternating treatment design." Also this form of design is useful for determining which of two alternative treatments is more effective. There is no need to return to a baseline or to withdraw treatment as is the case, for example, with the A-B-A design.

Another limitation of this design results from the need to use behaviors that can change quite rapidly, as the treatment changes. If an individual cannot quickly shift behavior this design is not appropriate for use. There may also be "sequential confounding" and/or "carryover" problems connected with this design.

Changing Criteria Design

This design uses an initial baseline followed by a treatment, just as the A-B design does. The "changing criterion design," however, continues to use the same treatment during the "B" phase until an established criterion is met. The design can be represented symbolically as A-B-B^1-B^2-B^3-B^4-B^n. Once behavior during the "B" phase has stabilized, if the change has not reached a final desired level of performance, a new and more stringent criterion is established. The first treatment (B) phase serves as the baseline for using the same treatment during a second treatment or "B^1" phase. The design calls for continued treatments with increasingly more demanding criteria until the client has been moved either close to, or has achieved, an ultimate goal. Treatment, for example, is carried out during the "B^1" phase until the behavior becomes stable. If, however, the behavior has not achieved the desired criterion, then the "B^1" phase serves as a baseline for an even more stringent criterion to be met during a follow-up treatment phase using the same treatment and labeled the "B^2" phase. This increase in rigorousness of criterion continues in a step fashion with the same treatment being used until the behavior achieves the criterion level that has been established by the practitioner.

Figure 2-6 illustrates an example using the "changing criterion design" with a problem of nail biting.

The baseline "A" shows that the subject displayed an average of 50 minutes of nail biting during six hours of observation for six days.

Each successive treatment required a drop of 10% from the previous phase. Thus, to meet the first treatment (B) criterion, the overall observations for B had to average 10% less nail biting, or 45 minutes, compared to the baseline (A) which averaged 50 minutes. Similarly, the second treatment (B^1) required a criterion of 10% less nail biting than the first treatment (B). To meet criterion the average number of minutes of nail biting during the B^1 phase had to be approximately 40 minutes. As can be seen from Figure 2-6 each successive treatment met the required criterion resulting in the nail biting being reduced to an average of approximately 30 minutes during the B^4 treatment phase covering days 30 to 36.

The changing criterion design is one that allows the research-practitioner to establish a desired outcome of targeted behavior and to continue to intensify the treatment to achieve that goal. The presumption underlying this design is that the treatment or intervention will work and can have cumulative effects that will help the client to move in a desired direction. By increasing the number of interventions an even more preferable goal of behavior can be obtained over time.

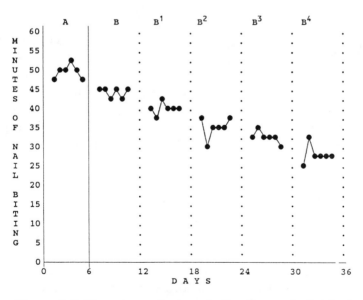

Figure 2-6 Changing criterion design for an individual
with a severe nail biting problem.

Advantages and Disadvantages of the Changing Criteria Design

When a clinician is interested in gradually changing behavior over time the "changing criteria design" is quite useful. Since the treatment continues to be applied over time the desired targeted behavior may reach a level that might not be feasible with other designs where less treatment time does not permit for continued improvement. The baseline data obtained when using a "changing criteria design" should be relatively stable and should not indicate change that is moving in the direction opposite to what the intervention will hopefully accomplish.

Also, it is important for the practitioner to establish a realistic end goal toward which behavioral change will be directed. To accomplish the final goal, the worker must decide on a reasonable length of time to conduct the study in order to achieve that goal. The number of treatments to be given throughout the study also needs to be considered as well as a decision about what constitutes an achievable criterion for each phase. These are not easy decisions to make and they must be made while constantly keeping the therapeutic needs of the client in mind.

Causality, attributing the treatment to the achievement of the final goal, is not easily established with the changing criteria design. Although Hartmann and Hall (1976) recommended that satisfactory completion of a study using this design could be achieved when the final behavioral goal was accomplished twice, Kratochwill (1978) advocated that treatment should be replicated at least four times to establish that the treatment had indeed achieved the initially established ultimate goal.

Because the changing criteria design is extended over many treatment phases, history as a threat to internal validity, becomes a serious problem. Results may be influenced by changing conditions in the environment during the experimental treatment.

Multiple Baseline Designs

Multiple baseline designs are generally used when: (1) the clinician has a single client with more than one problem, or (2) there are two or more clients who have a similar type of problem, or (3) there are two or more settings that involve the same problem. After a baseline phase the treatment variable is used for two or more individuals, behaviors, or situations.

When using the multiple baselines across individuals, a clinician would establish baselines on similar behaviors, in the same setting, for two or more clients and would then examine the extent of change from each of the baseline behaviors after using the same treatment. For example three different individuals, with problems of excessive gambling, might be given a specific form of counseling therapy to see whether the counseling helped to reduce the gambling problem for each of these individuals. Figure 2-7 shows what the multiple baseline design for this research would look like. Note that the baselines A_1, A_2 and A_3 all begin at the same time for each of the individuals, but while Mr. Abel's baseline observations are terminated and treatment is begun after the fourth day the other two individuals are observed through more extended baseline periods. Baselines and treatment phases can easily be seen as conceptualizations of the A-B design where three clients are exposed to the same treatment under "time-lagged" conditions. With the "multiple baseline design" the length of the baselines increase for each succeeding client. When the clinician-researcher can

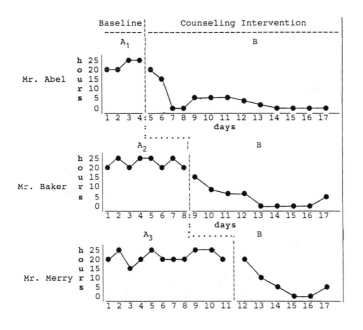

Figure 2-7 Multiple baselines showing hours per day of gambling for three compulsive gamblers.

see changes occur, as is the case shown by the graph of the compulsive gamblers where gambling time dropped dramatically, he or she has some degree of confidence that the treatment has produced a beneficial effect upon the clients' behavior. It can be seen that throughout all of the baselines for each individual the rate of gambling was maintained at a rather high level, but as soon as the counseling treatment was introduced gambling time dropped appreciably.

For the multiple baselines across behaviors, a clinician would establish baselines for two or more behaviors, in the same setting, for the same client and would examine the extent of change in behavior from each baseline as the result of the same treatment. For example, a baseline period for an emotionally immature child could be established using temper tantrums, food throwing and screaming as three undesirable behaviors. The same treatment would then be used for each behavioral problem under study to see if the treatment reduced the undesirable behaviors in the one child.

For multiple baselines across situations, if a clinician found that a treatment changed a particular baseline behavior in a client in a given setting then the same client would be placed into a second setting to see if the treatment would again change the client's behavior from baseline in the second setting. The same procedure would be used to test the response of the client to the treatment in a third setting. The situations in this type of design can vary considerably such as different time periods or different physical locations.

Advantages and Disadvantages of the Multiple Baseline Design

The Multiple Baseline Design allows a practitioner to feel some degree of confidence in drawing cause and effect conclusions about a treatment because the treatment can be applied to several behaviors in the same person, to several clients using the same treatment, or to several settings for the same individual. This type of design helps to control for more of the threats to internal validity than is true for the basic A-B design or even for the withdrawal designs.

One of the problems with the "multiple baseline design" is that clients must be treated in a sequential orderly fashion. Unfortunately, clients sometimes need assistance which is not in consonance with the requirements of this design. For example, if either Mr. Merry or Mr. Baker would have needed help before the end of their baseline phases the implementation of this design would not have been feasible. The client's needs must always be kept uppermost in mind.

Another problem with this design is that it may not be easy to find three or more clients with similar enough problems to make comparisons or with comparable characteristics that would make them amenable to the same treatment. In addition, the design requires a relatively stable baseline which may not be easily attainable. Sometimes baseline data shows considerable variability and in such instances the "multiple baseline design" is not suitable for use. One last problem associated with the "multiple baseline design" is that the effects of the first treatment on the individual's behavior may in some way carry over and influence the results obtained for the second or third treatment. These limitations should be kept in mind when using this design.

CHAPTER 3

GRAPHING METHODOLOGY

Information collected from clients during baseline and treatment phases can be, and often is, placed into tables. Such data in tabular form, however, may not be as easily described as when the data are placed into a graph. Graphing, normally involves plotting information collected from both baseline and treatment phases onto graph paper. Once the data have been graphed, then changes from baseline to treatment can be seen.

TWO METHODS OF DATA ANALYSIS

There are essentially two processes that can be applied to analyze single subject data. One is by means of quantitative analysis, which includes the use of statistics. The other is by visual interpretation or graphing. Before the beginning of single subject statistical testing, graphing was, and even today still is, the primary method of analysis (Kratochwill, et al., 1984; Hudson, 1977). Although they are quite different, both methods are concerned with errors in interpretation of the data that could lead a research-practitioner to draw erroneous conclusions. All traditional forms of statistical tests seek to eliminate error or bias by requiring randomness. Randomness, includes *random selection* or *random assignment*. The merits behind randomness, for group types of analyses, certainly cannot be questioned. When little is actually known about the effect of study variables it is logical to proceed by trying to eliminate any initial biases that might be present to avoid bias in the end results. Random selection attempts to prevent the prejudicial choosing of subjects by making sure that every individual in the population has had an equal opportunity to be selected. Random assignment also tries to reduce bias that might occur by virtue of subjects being preferentially placed into one group or another.

For single subject research, however, the idea behind random selection or random assignment of subjects is not tenable because there is only one subject to study. Instead of relying on randomness to reduce error, single subject studies attempt to reduce bias by requiring the systematic replication of conditions based upon the greatest possible precision and reliability of measurement methods. Thus, researchers and practitioners using single subject analysis try to understand the nature of the changes that occur and strive to select replication procedures that will strengthen the confirmation of findings that have been obtained.

Both visual interpretations and statistics have their strengths and weaknesses. Neither are the "be-all and end-all" for examining data. Both must be conceived as co-methods to be applied with discretion. There may be times when graphing will provide the needed information and there may be other times when statistical analysis may be the preferable choice.

GRAPHING INFORMATION FOR STUDIES ON HUMAN BEHAVIOR

Graphs can be very helpful for explaining, interpreting and analyzing information obtained from studying human behavior. Graphs use points, lines, areas, and geometric forms as the major methods for providing meaningful conclusions. With graphs quantifiable data, such as trends or relationships, can be clearly, simply and understandably presented. Some of the merits for charts and graphs are:

1. They provide a very important means of visual communication. If well made graphs can depict information more clearly and parsimoniously than might be obtainable from data set forth in table format.

2. They may be timesavers because a good deal of data can be quickly visualized at a glance.

3. They can serve as a stimulus for analytical thinking which at times can enhance the research process.

Anyone with a serious interest in single subject research should be knowledgeable about the principles of constructing graphs. Although graphing techniques are an important and effective method for presenting data, they are not under all circumstances and for all purposes complete substitutes for either table or statistical presentations. Graphing techniques also have their limitations as explained beginning on page 38. The practitioner-researcher should be aware of these weaknesses, in order to become adept at using graphing methods to accurately display information.

USING THE POLYGON AS A GRAPHING TECHNIQUE

The origin of graphing is most likely traceable to William Playfair who, in 1798, published a book entitled *The Commercial and Political Atlas*. In the book referring to "lineal arithmetic" he said:

The advantage proposed by this method, is not that of giving a more accurate statement than by figures, but it is to give a more simple and permanent idea of the gradual progress and comparative amounts, at different periods, by presenting to the eye a figure, the proportions of which correspond with the amount of the sums intended to be expressed. (Playfair, 1798, pp. ix–x)

Thus, Playfair's description about graphs was so well expressed that his knowledge compares favorably with present day graphing techniques. He discussed what is presently the best known type of graph, called a "polygon."

Polygons are also known as "line," "rectilinear," "rectangular," or "Cartesian coordinate" graphs. They are so named because they are developed by plotting data on a coordinate surface in which the successive points are joined together to form a continuous line. The line drawn between successive points may be smooth, but not necessarily and, in fact, is often angular. The system of coordinates in polygons is based upon two intersecting lines called "axes." The horizontal line is called the "X-axis" or the "abscissa" and the vertical line is called the "Y-axis" or the "ordinate." The X-axis generally represents the independent variable and is frequently seen in time units such as seconds, minutes, hours, days, etc. The Y-axis usually represents the dependent variable, which is the amount or the criteria by which the independent variable is being evaluated. These axes divide the plane of the coordinate into four equal parts called "quadrants," which are numbered counterclockwise, beginning with the upper right quadrant. Figure 3-1 shows a Cartesian coordinate which represents the basic form for all graphs.

The point at which the X or abscissa axis and the Y or ordinate axis intersect, labeled 0, is called the "point of origin." All measurements to the right and above the point of origin are positive values and all measurements to the left and below the point of origin are negative numbers. Both the X- and Y-axes can be divided into any desired units of measurement, beginning with the point of origin as zero. A point plotted in any quadrant is determined by whether the two numbers representing that point are positive or negative as well as the distances of the numbers on both the X- and Y-axes. In Figure 3-1, for example, point **P**, representing two numbers has been located at $Y = +2$ and $X = +6$. With descriptive graphing, Quadrant I is used almost exclusively, but on occasion when negative numbers are to be plotted Quadrant II or IV may also be used. Quadrant III represents a rare entity in graphing and is seldom used.

The *polygon* is particularly effective for portraying observations obtained from time series designs. It lends itself to representing movements or trends over time periods which may include hours, days, weeks, months or years. There is another form sometimes used for

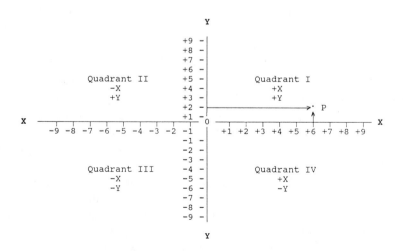

Figure 3-1 A Cartesian Coordinate graph

graphing observations over time, called a *bar graph*, which will be discussed shortly.

When selecting a particular type of graph to use with longitudinal data, consideration should be given to the meaning of the data, the problem at hand, the purpose of the chart and the audience to whom the graph is being directed. There really is no "best" graphing method and all forms have their advantages and disadvantages.

Essential Components of a Polygon

When using a polygon, the title, the form of scaling and the nature of the grid proportions must be considered. Each of these factors will be discussed briefly.

Title

The title of a graph is usually placed at the top, on the outside of the graph itself. This is generally the format used not only for a polygon, but also for all other types of graphs. There are times when the title is located under the graph, but that usually happens when explanations are given about the graph. When the title is placed under the graph it is often bold faced and of the same type size as found in the balance of the document. When the title is at the top of the graph the letter size used in the title is often larger than any other type used in the graph. The title should present to the reader information about (1) what the study was about, (2) where the study took place, and (3) when the study was conducted. It is inadvisable for the title of a graph to be more than three lines long and it should never contain abbreviated words unless they are standard and generally accepted by the reading audience.

Scaling

It was mentioned earlier that the unit of time is usually placed on the abscissa. Normally graphs follow a time sequence in which the earliest data are plotted at the left and later data are plotted on the right. Plotting information for the independent variable may seem easy and straightforward but that will not be true unless the variable has been clearly defined. Take for example the time unit "days." The term "day" can be interpreted in several ways. It might be the "awake period of a day" for a child, it could be a "24-hour day," or even a "work day." It might also be interpreted as being a "daylight day" between sunrise and sunset. The time unit should be clearly stated so the reader of the graph understands what the creator is attempting to convey. Figure 3-2 shows only quadrant I of a Cartesian coordinate because all of the values both for the abscissa and the ordinate are positive. The graph depicts the ordinate as the frequency of the behavior while the abscissa is shown as daily time units.

Note that the zero, which indicates no occurrence of the behavior has been placed on the ordinate, but the location of the zero on the X- or Y-axis is arbitrary and depends on whether the creator of the graph believes that a more clear picture might be presented if the zero was located on the abscissa. Usually, there is greater clarity of presentation if the zero is placed on the ordinate.

Grid Proportions

Creating the grid for a polygon requires that care be taken to assure that a proper balance exists for the scales that are used. A graph may be correct in every detail, but badly proportioned. There are no hard and fast rules for establishing appropriate proportions for any given graph. Usually the best thing to do is to graph the data and then look at the graph to make sure that it appears to be representative of the data.

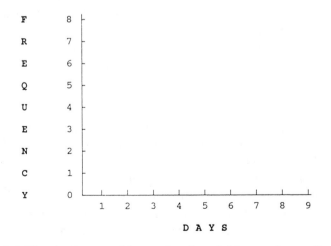

Figure 3-2 The frequency (dependent) variable on the ordinate and the time (independent) variable on the abscissa.

While the *polygon* or *line graph* has rather extensive use in providing pictorial presentations of data there is another form of graph that is also appropriate for time series observations. It is called the *bar graph* or sometimes a *column graph*.

USING THE BAR GRAPH

The bar graph provides a way to represent data that have usually been obtained in the form of categories or classes. A bar is drawn for each category, in which the height of the bar indicates the frequency that is found in each particular class or category. One example of categorical data might be days, such as the first, second, third, fourth, and fifth day.

Some authors distinguish between a bar graph and a column graph. They call a graph with horizontal bars emanating from the ordinate, a bar graph as opposed to bars arising from the abscissa which is called a column graph.

The bar graph is suitable for time series data as long as a large number of bars are not needed. A bar graph is the easiest type of graph to prepare and use in reporting data. It is also readily understood by those with little or no research background. If there are a considerable number of bars to be displayed, the graph may appear cluttered. When creating a bar graph all the bars should be uniform in width. The spacing between the bars is arbitrary, but usually the amount of space will vary from half of the bar width to the full size of the width of the bar. For comparison of magnitudes of difference, the bar graph provides a precise and accurate impression.

As an example of a bar graph, the number of one client's baseline tics were counted. The observations were taken during three randomly selected time periods of 15 minutes each for five days. The tics displayed by this individual were quick and abrupt movements that included blinking, grimacing, shaking or nodding the head. Figure 3-3 shows a bar graph containing information on the average frequencies of tics over the five day period.

The bar graph in Figure 3-3 shows that the number of tics displayed during the three daily observational periods were essentially the same over the five day span. On the first day the individual had 63 tics, day two 70 tics, days three and four 63, and day five 60.

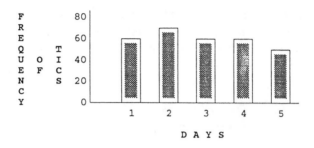

Figure 3-3 Baseline data showing the mean number of tics displayed during three daily 15-minute observations over a five day period.

GRAPHS THAT ARE DECEIVING

While the creator of a graph is given considerable latitude, if a graph is not drawn properly, it can give visual distortions. Proper standards of graph preparation allow the graph maker to omit selected parts, such as the breaking of a grid. The viewer should be alert to broken bars or broken ordinates because they can give an appearance that is easily misunderstood or misinterpreted. Note in Figure 3-4(a) that the broken bar makes a sizable jump from the baseline of 0 to 1000. The viewer gets the impression that the difference between the two bars is really greater than it actually is. Looking at the unbroken bars in Figure 3-4(b) the differential between them is considerably diminished.

Another type of bar graph visual distortion occurs when the abscissa

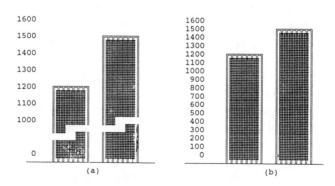

Figure 3-4 Exaggeration of difference between a broken bar compared to a continuous bar.

is displaced below the zero point on the graph. Depressing the abscissa has the effect of accentuating the height of the bars. Figure 3-5(a) shows a graph with the abscissa below the zero point while Figure 3-5(b) shows the data plotted at the zero point of the abscissa.

A broken ordinate axis that is shown in Figure 3-6 also indicates how easy it is to distort a polygon graph and thus give the reader a mistaken impression. Notice how the polygon in Figure 3-6(a), where the axis has been broken and the values from 1 to 20 have been skipped, exaggerates the difference between the two lines. The degree of misrepresentation can be seen by comparing Figure 3-6(a) with the unbroken axis in Figure 3-6(b). The small difference is readily discernable when the ordinate axis has been left intact.

Sometimes graph makers do not even break the bar or the ordinate axis but merely show the units without a zero. If this is done considerable distortion can be occur, as exemplified in the bar graph of Figure 3-7.

When it comes to designing polygons one of the most difficult problems is to determine what size units to use on the two axes. The decision about unit size is highly subjective, but it is definitely one that will

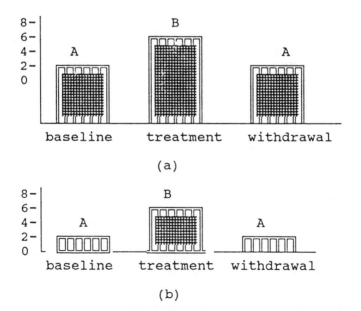

Figure 3-5 Depressed abscissa resulting in visual distortion.

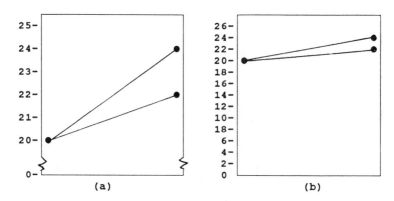

Figure 3-6 Two polygons plotted with the same data, except that one has a broken ordinate which exaggerates the differences between the two lines.

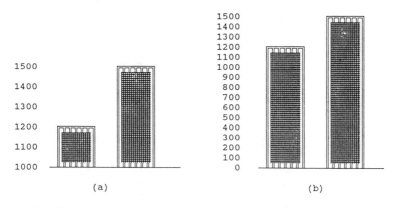

Figure 3-7 Exaggeration of difference between a bars without a zero compared to those where the zero is shown.

influence the appearance of the graph. If the scale on the horizontal axis is spread and the vertical units are compressed, the line will flatten out. This is in contrast to the situation where the vertical axis is spread and the horizontal axis is compressed, thus making the line appear to rise dramatically. Figure 3-8(a) when compared to Figure 3-8(b) shows how the appearance of the same data can look so different when the axes are compressed or spread.

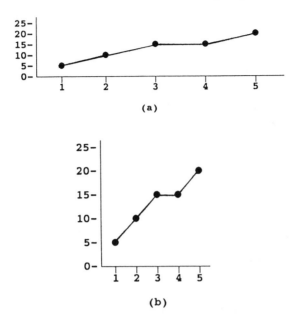

Figure 3-8 Two polygon graphs with different spreads of units on ordinate and abscissa axes, demonstrating how the same plotted data can look quite different.

STEPS FOR GRAPHING SINGLE SUBJECTS

Before any graphing of baseline data can begin, a precise description of the behavior that is being targeted for change, must be developed and written. The description should be sufficiently specific so that if more than one observer is used they will be in close agreement when recording the same behavior. A pretest of inter-observer reliability should be performed and agreements should be at least 80% or better (Kazdin, 1975). Once the behavior has been clearly defined and there is inter-observer agreement, there are four recommended sequential steps for establishing a graphic illustration of a single subject study. They are: (1) gather and plot the baseline data, (2) examine the baseline data, (3) record the treatment data, and (4) interpret the data at the point where the baseline ends and the treatment begins. The following brief discussion is pertinent to each of these steps.

1. **Gather and plot the baseline data.** The first step in developing a graph for analysis is to observe the targeted behavior and plot it on

a graph as baseline data. Often baseline information will be gathered during the diagnostic stage of clinical treatment. While the baseline is generally referred to as the "no treatment" phase of single subject research, the "no treatment" does not mean that nothing is being done for the client. The "A" or "no treatment" phase simply means that the intervention that will be used following the baseline period to help the client is not used during the baseline.

Once the criteria for evaluating the outcome variable have been decided, then a systematic graphing of baseline information should be undertaken. Baseline data generally precede the intervention or treatment so the researcher can visually determine whether there has been a change in the behavior once the treatment has been introduced.

Sometimes the best interests of the client are not served by delaying a treatment. In such instances if previously obtained figures are on record they may be used as baseline information. It is always better, however, to use the most recent data available.

Another unresolved issue about collecting baseline information is the length of time and the number of observations to make. There is no such thing as an agreed upon correct length of time or number of observations. Hersen and Barlow (1976) suggested at least three data points to determine a baseline trend, although Gingerich (1979) wrote that a minimum of 10 observations is necessary to begin to see a natural pattern in the data. Much depends upon the type of design that is being used, the nature of the problem, the needs of the client and the variability or instability in the baseline data.

It is also important to try to detect whether an emerging pattern can be seen. A distinguishing pattern of behavior during baseline is important because visual interpretation of graphed single subject data is based upon a comparison between the baseline and the treatment phase.

2. **Examine the baseline data.** Since the first step was the creation of a baseline, the second is to look at the data to see if there is some discernable configuration. Inspecting the baseline data serves the purpose of helping the researcher to understand what the baseline is like and to see if any pattern of the targeted behavior can be observed. Unless a clear baseline pattern does emerge, there is a potential for possible error when making comparisons between the baseline and the treatment phases. An important characteristic of

the baseline that should be considered is the degree of steadiness of the data.

Constancy of Direction

A *constant pathway*, also called a "trend" or "slope," is one that moves directionally in a relatively steady fashion. Figure 3-9 shows a stylized graph of three forms of steady baselines. The "a" line represents a steadily increasing pattern, the "b" line displays steadiness of the data without either positive or negative direction, and the "c" line depicts a steadily decreasing data pattern. Baseline data with constancy in direction, indicate less random variation than data that does not have consistent directionality.

The direction in which the data are moving is also important. If the baseline data are moving steadily in a direction that would represent an improvement in the client's behavior as the result of treatment, it is much more difficult to claim that the treatment had an effect since the data were already moving in the desired direction. For example, if a practitioner was able to reduce an undesirable behavior as shown in Figure 3-9 during the treatment phase, the change would not be nearly as dramatic if the baseline behavior was already moving downward, as exemplified by line "c." It would be difficult to claim that the treatment really had much of an effect. On the other hand, if the baseline for the undesirable behavior

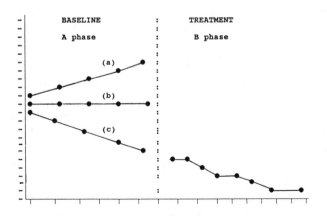

Figure 3-9 Steady baseline date are represented by all three lines but "c" does not show the degree of change that "a" or "b" would indicate if a treatment were to reduce a particular behavior.

looked like either line "b" or especially line "a" and during the treatment phase the undesirable behavior declined, then it could be more readily assumed that the treatment was producing an obvious reduction in the client's undesirable behavior.

Variability

A baseline that displays considerable variability is not useful because it does not provide for a clear understanding of the nature of the behavior and it cannot be visually projected into the treatment phase of the research. If the behavior that is being observed oscillates erratically, then little can be said about the characteristics of the behavior except, of course, that the observed behavior varies. Until less variability and more stability can be seen in the baseline observations, it is difficult to interpret what effect the treatment might have had on the client. When a client's behavior is excessively errant there are at least two actions that a clinician may take. First, sometimes just waiting for a short time may result in the development of a more stable pattern of the targeted behavior. Second, a brief clinical assessment might give clues as to what may be producing the erratic behavior in the client. Perhaps the client is encountering either psychological or environmental conflicts during the baseline phase which, in turn, may be creating a highly irregular frequency of the behavior. Taking a baseline at a more propititious time, or at least being alert to what might be causing the variability of behavior, could perhaps lead to observations that would be much more stable and, therefore, more useful. Figure 3-10 shows three baselines with variability in the data.

Figure 3-10(a) shows a pattern with considerable variability over the entire baseline period. Since no underlying pattern is discernable from this baseline, its use would be questionable for comparing with a treatment phase. Figure 3-10(b) shows a beginning steady baseline but the baseline then moves toward instability. This baseline also has too much variability at the conclusion of the baseline observations to be useful although it started with a clearly steady pattern. Figure 3-10(c) displays instability of the baseline in the beginning observations and later levels off to become steady. While Figure 3-10(c) might provide a usable baseline of information, it would be important to try to ascertain what caused the instability during the early part of the baseline.

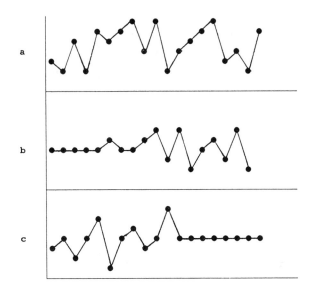

Figure 3-10 Three forms of unsteadiness in baseline data

3. **Record the treatment data.** Now that the baseline data have been gathered and scrutinized it is time to begin treatment and record the data. Data should be continuously recorded during treatment. The information obtained while in the treatment phase should be plotted on the same graph immediately following the baseline data. There should be a line of demarcation separating the two phases to show at what point the treatment was introduced.

4. **Interpret the data at the point where the baseline ends and the treatment begins.** Up to now the discussion has focused on "within phase" strategies. These strategies are concerned with data found within a particular phase, exemplified either by the baseline or the treatment phase. Strategies, however, are also concerned with "between phases" such as what occurs to the behavior being studied at the point when the baseline stops and the treatment begins.

There are two conditions in which change can occur at the point between the end of the baseline phase and the beginning of the first treatment. These conditions are called *level* and *direction*. Level refers to a change in frequency of the behavior between the baseline and the treatment. Direction indicates whether an immediate change in the projected course of the behavior has occurred at the exact point of intervention. Figure 3-11 shows several ways in which level and direction can be interpreted.

Figure 3-11(a) where there has been an immediate change in both direction and level between phases, gives a convincing impression,

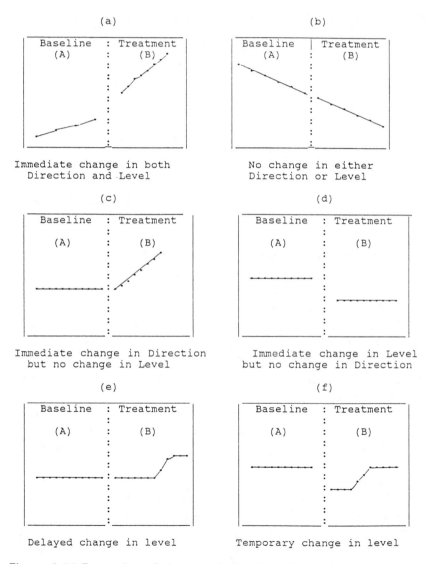

Figure 3-11 Examples of changes in level and direction at the point of treatment intervention.

if, for example, the intent of the treatment was to increase the frequency of the behavior. Generally the greater and steeper the change in both level and direction the more convincing the data will appear (Parsonson and Baer, 1978).

Figure 3-11(b) shows a decreasing, but stable baseline that displays no change in either direction or level. When this type of stability exist it permits for predicability from the baseline through the intervention phase.

Figure 3-11(c) shows an immediate change in direction from the baseline which is sometimes labeled an "abrupt" change in direction. If there is an abrupt change in direction, as shown in this Figure, the researcher might be wise to continue monitoring and recording more extended treatment observations. There is a possibility that such an abrupt change in behavior may reverse itself and begin returning to its original level.

Figure 3-11(d) shows no change in direction, but a very "abrupt" change in level. Again, as was stated previously, such an abrupt change in level appears to provide convincing evidence that the treatment had a "true" effect.

Figure 3-11(e) shows a delayed change in behavior while Figure 3-11(f) shows that changes in behavior at the point of intervention may be immediate, but temporary. On occasion, the behavior changes shown in Figure 3-11(e) may extinguish and revert to the original baseline level after a period of time.

In summary, there are no rigid qualifying rules for interpretation of changes that occur from baseline to treatment phases. Changes may be immediate, delayed, temporary or permanent and may appear as a shift in level or direction. Each of these changes should be closely examined and interpreted with caution.

DETERMINING LINEAR DIRECTION
OF A DISTRIBUTION

Graphing the directionality of data can be done in one of three ways. One method is to view the data points and then draw a straight line in what seems to be the best fit through all of the plotted points. Obviously, reliability of such a line is subject to real question. One person might draw the line through the points in a different manner than another. The freehand drawing of a line through the data is subjective and generally is not a suitably representative directional line.

Another somewhat more reliable approach than the first, is to take a given phase such as the baseline, divide it in half and then calculate the mean for each half. The two means are then plotted on the ordinate where the midpoint of each half of the phase lies. Once the two points have been plotted a straight line is drawn through both points. This line will indicate the directional path of the data through the various data points. While helpful it is not considered to be a fully dependable estimate of the directional course of the data because only two averaged points are used.

By comparison with the two previous procedures for establishing the best pathway line through graphed data the most accurate is the third method, called a *Regression Line*. It uses all the individual data points that are found in a distribution. The Regression method, used primarily for predicting the values of an unknown variable from a known variable, also provides the basis for assessing the directional nature of data. A regression line can be calculated for the "A" phase (baseline) or for the "B" (treatment) phase.

With the regression method, a mathematical fit of a line is made through the scatter of dots on a graph. This line is also called a *Best Fit Line* or the *Least Squares Line* because it fits best when the squared deviations of all the observation points from the line are smaller than the distance from any other line that could be drawn through the graph. The line is also referred to as a *Regression Line*. The squared deviations

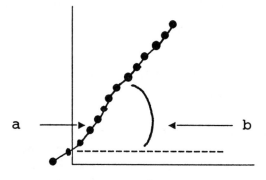

Figure 3-12 In regression analysis "a" represents height and "b" indicates the slope of the line.

can be taken either horizontally or vertically depending on which variable is considered the independent variable.

The formula for the straight regression line is $Y = a + bX$; where, "Y" is the value of the variable that is to be estimated, "a" is the height of the line where it crosses the Y axis, and b is the slope or inclination of the line.

The regression formula provides information about the exact position of the Least Squares Line. To find the values for "a" and "b" two formulas are used. They are:

$$b = \frac{(N)(\sum XY) - (\sum X)(\sum Y)}{(N)(\sum X^2) - (\sum X)^2}$$

$$a = \frac{(\sum Y) - (b \sum X)}{N}$$

Information on X and Y values shown in Figure 3-13 will be used to determine the height ("a") and slope ("b") of the Least Squares Line. It should be obvious to the reader that the four data points being used are an artifically small number of observations in order to maintain simplicity and for ease in understanding the regression process.

The data found in Figure 3-13 have been placed into tabular form in Table 3-1 and summed values for X, X^2, Y and XY from the table are then substituted into the formula for the calculation of "b." Similarly

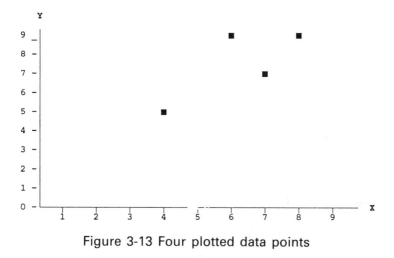

Figure 3-13 Four plotted data points

Table 3-1 Calculation of Linear Pathway through Observed Values by Means of a Least Squares Line

X	X^2	Y	XY
6	36	9	54
7	49	7	49
8	64	9	72
4	16	5	20
$\Sigma X = 25$	$\Sigma X^2 = 165$	$\Sigma Y = 30$	$\Sigma XY = 195$

$N = 4$

$$b = \frac{(N)(\Sigma XY) - (\Sigma X)(\Sigma Y)}{(N)(\Sigma X^2) - (\Sigma X)^2}$$

$$b = \frac{(4)(195) - (25)(30)}{(4)(165) - (25)^2}$$

$$b = \frac{780 - 750}{660 - 625}$$

$$b = \frac{30}{35}$$

$$b = .857$$

$$a = \frac{\Sigma Y - b\,\Sigma X}{N} \qquad \text{Substitute the above calculated}$$
value for "b" here.

$$a = \frac{30 - (.857)(25)}{4}$$

$$a = \frac{30 - 21.425}{4}$$

$$a = \frac{8.575}{4}$$

$$a = 2.144$$

"a" is calculated by using the sums of X and Y and substituting in the predetermined value of "b."

Now it is necessary to go back to the regression formula which was:

$$Y = a + bX$$

Substituting the value of "a" which was 2.144 and "b" which was .857 into the equation and placing any value for X, let us say 5, into the formula provides the following estimated value for Y. This value based upon the known selected value of 5, is then inserted into the Y formula.

$$Y = 2.144 + (.857)(X)$$
$$Y = 2.144 + (.857)(5)$$
$$Y = 2.144 + 4.285$$
$$Y = 6.429$$

Any other values for X, which for this example would be values from 4 to 8, that fall within the X distribution, could be inserted into the Y formula to obtain an estimated value of Y. The estimated value of Y for the point on X that would be equal to the mean of X, which is symbolized as $(\overline{X})$, is $b(X - \overline{X})$. The formula $b(X - \overline{X})$ is equal to zero and, therefore, Y is equal to the mean of Y symbolized as $(\overline{Y})$. Thus, one point on the "least squares" line will always go through the mean of X and the mean of Y, in this case 6.25 and 7.5.

Based upon the information that is now available for a known value of X, as well as the means of both X and Y, a straight line on a graph can be drawn which is called the "regression line." Figure 3-14 shows the line.

Regression, then, is the name of a method that provides information about the path of a straight line through the marked observation values that have been entered on a graph. The line can be called a "Best Fit Line," a "Least Squares Line," or a "Regression Line." Each of

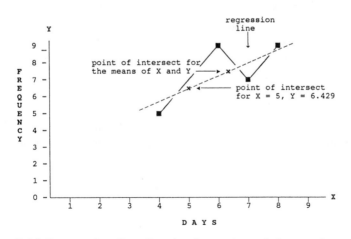

Figure 3-14 Regression line for the four plotted data points shown in Figure 3-13.

these names represents the same line. This method for determining the direction of a line through a series of plotted points on a graph is superior to the "eyeballing method" of visually trying to draw a line through the dotted points or the "averaging method" previously described.

USING A REGRESSION ANALYSIS TO DETERMINE THE IMPACT OF TREATMENT

Up to this point the discussion has focused on the use of statistical regression to determine the direction of a line within a particular phase when plotted through data. However, regression analysis has also been suggested for analyzing the effectiveness of the treatment when the baseline regression is projected through the treatment phase (Kelly, McNeil and Newman, 1973; Kaestner and Ross, 1974). The regression line drawn through the treatment or B phase is viewed as being particularly impressive if, as is anticipated, the frequency of treatment observations fall above (or below) the projected line. If the intent of the research is to reduce a specific behavior and the behavior falls below the projected regression line, the visual impression would seem to indicate a fair level of success. The same would be true in the opposite direction, if the behavior was considered successfully treated when it fell above the projected regression line.

There has been some confusion in the literature about the statistical analysis connected with interpreting whether the observational changes during treatment can be considered to be significantly different from the baseline period, when relying on a regression line. The confusion has centered primarily around the autocorrelated data and it is recommended that a regression line should not be used for determining statistically significant difference if the data are serially dependent. Therefore, before attempting to use a regression line for predicting future behavior the data should be analyzed for autocorrelation, as described on page 58.

CHAPTER 4

STATISTICS FOR
SINGLE SUBJECT DESIGNS

As stated previously when traditional group type statistics are used for analyzing single subject data several factors may adversely affect the statistic and its capability to handle violations (robustness) presented by the data. One of the violations that no inferential statistic can tolerate is for the data to be serially dependent (Scheffe, 1959; Toothaker, Banz, Noble, Camp, and Davis, 1983).

ADVANTAGES AND DISADVANTAGES OF
STATISTICAL ANALYSIS OF SINGLE SUBJECTS

Some researchers believe that statistics are unnecessary for studying a single case (Skinner, 1966). There are a few others who feel that certain inferential statistics can be used to interpret the effect of a treatment regardless of the degree of serial dependency. Most, including this author, believe that classical inferential statistics are not appropriate for single case studies unless there is some degree of assurance that problems resulting from evaluating successive observations have been considered.

Group type statistics require the assumption of independence of observations. For their proper use subjects must be either randomly selected, randomly assigned, or matched on some particular variable. Because these limitations cannot be reasonably applied to a single subject who is being studied, even if significance of difference were to be found employing the accepted forms of group statistics, the results of the analysis would probably be unreliable. Error could result from an artifact of the statistic itself producing inaccurate information about the effectiveness or ineffectiveness of the treatment.

Under the discussion of graphing in Chapter 3, it was stated that before the development of some of the current statistical approaches for analyzing single case data, graphs were and today still are, the main method for determining whether a particular treatment for a subject has had any effect (Parsonson and Baer, 1978; Sidman, 1960; Hudson, 1977). Regardless of whether it is graphing or statistical analysis, researchers using either of these procedures are hopeful that they can avoid both alpha and beta errors.* An *alpha* error results if a decision is made that the treatment produced a genuine effect when in fact the result was really a chance factor that was operating and was not due to the treatment at all. A *beta* error occurs if a decision is made that the treatment did *not* produce a genuine effect when in truth it really did. When data are graphed the researcher visually inspects the plotted information, but cannot actually determine whether or not the treatment produced a "genuine" effect. The plotted data may look as though the treatment was either effective or ineffective but either way the researcher cannot be certain, within reasonable levels of probability, that his or her decision was correct (DeProspero and Cohen, 1979; Furlong and Wampold, 1981, Jones, Vaught, and Weinrott, 1977). Thus, statistical decision errors cannot be determined on the bases of graphed data.

The only real way that the researcher can feel assured that he or she is not making an error is to base decisions on highly consistent changes in results. By holding out for such consistent information a researcher can reduce the probability of making an alpha error, but would certainly increase the chance of making a beta error, since these two forms of errors are inversely related to each other. Those researchers who seek strongly consistent results, which they read visually from a graph, are more likely to commit a beta error compared to those who use some form of statistical analysis.

In the past statistical procedures for single subject analysis were used when the results of an intervention could not be easily interpreted. If a treatment provided considerable improvement in the client's behavior, statistical testing was not considered necessary. The concept "considerable improvement," however, is difficult to interpret and as stated previously a problem arises trying to define "considerable." On the other hand some lesser results were thought to be questionable because

*Note: See Krishef, C. H., *Fundamental Statistics for Human Services and Social Work* for a complete discussion of Alpha and Beta errors.

they were difficult to interpret by graphing. Statistical examination was, therefore, regarded as beneficial for detecting relatively small but consistent effects produced by a treatment. Statistics provided research practitioners with formal, generally consistent criteria from which they could draw conclusions. There were also those workers who believed that even if only small effects could be detected by statistical analysis, such data would be helpful because the information obtained about one treatment with small effects might be combined with other approaches that might produce considerable improvement in desired client behavior.

Certain disadvantages exist for selected forms of statistical analysis. Some procedures such as the Box-Jenkins method of time series analysis require many observational data points. Often the practitioner does not have the luxury of time to obtain a large number of observations or the client's situation may dictate the need for far fewer observations than are required by the design. These factors could mitigate against the use of the Box-Jenkins procedure. Other statistics also have their disadvantages. For example, Revusky's R_n, which is explained in this book, requires certain assumptions, such as treatment effects not being reversable, at least four baseline observations, and the use of a "multiple baseline" as the only applicable design.

Although statistical analysis is advantageous because there is provision for statements of probability, most traditional statistics are untenable with serially related data. The question then is how to determine whether or not single subject data are autocorrelated or serially related.

AUTOCORRELATION OF DATA

There is a method of calculation which can be used to determine whether or not the values of a single subject study are serially dependent or **autocorrelated**. Correlation indicates that two variables are related to each other. If one variable is correlated with another, one variable can be used to predict the other. Prediction is possible because knowledge about one variable provides information about the other variable. If no relationship exists, predictability is seriously reduced. If the scores are found to be successively related to each other, where there is a correlation between scores, traditional group type statistics are not applicable. If the scores are found to be independent of each other, that is, not correlated with each other, then it may be reasonable to apply group type statistics. Using a procedure called Bartlett's r (or Bartlett's test), symbolized as r_k, it is possible to determine whether data are, or are not, autocorrelated.

Before reviewing the procedural steps for Bartlett's r, a caveat is in order. A baseline consisting of a minimum of seven, and preferably more observations, should be obtained to calculate an autocorrelation. If there are too few observations the results may spuriously show independence of data.

Determining Whether Data are Autocorrelated

If a column of numbers is arbitrarily selected and a list of the same paired numbers is set in another column alongside the first, the correlation would be perfect. Refer to Table 4-1. The correlation coefficient (r) calculated for the two columns of numbers shown in Table 4-1, would equal 1 because each paired number is identically the same.

If the values of the second column were moved down one from the first column, and then integrated with the first column, the combined column would then consist of what are called *lagged values* because each value from the second column would succeed (lag behind) each value from the first column. Table 4-2 depicts the shifting by one value of the numbers in the second column, as well as the combining of the shifted second column values into the first column.

It is now possible to correlate the single combined column made from the two previous ones to see if there is any relationship between the successive scores. This type of correlation of lagged values is called a **serial correlation** because values follow each other in a series. The relationship is also referred to as an **autocorrelation** because it rep-

Table 4-1 Correlation of Paired Numbers

	First Column	Second Column
First pair	6	6
Second pair	7	7
Third pair	8	8
Fourth pair	7	7
Fifth pair	8	8
Sixth pair	9	9
Seventh pair	10	10
Eighth pair	10	10
Ninth pair	9	9
Tenth pair	13	13
Eleventh pair	9	9
Twelfth pair	12	12

Table 4-2 Shifting and Combining of Second Column
Values with Values Found in the First Column.

Column 1	Column 2	Combined Pairs (or lagged values)
6	7	6, 7
7	8	7, 8
8	7	8, 7
7	8	7, 8
8	9	8, 9
9	10	9, 10
10	10	10, 10
10	9	10, 9
9	13	9, 13
13	9	13, 9
9	12	9, 12
12		

resents a correlation of a variable on itself. The autocorrelation technique can be used for any variable when information about that variable is recorded in a sequential fashion. Examples, might be traffic accidents, crime rates, store sales, an individual's test scores, or any other data that are listed in a series.

To bring this discussion into sharper focus the values shown in column 1 of Table 4-1 represent the number of undesirable behaviors that were observed in 12 half-hour baseline periods during one week of observation of an eight-year old acting-out child. This is the "A" portion of the "A-B" design. Observations of the child's behavior were made during randomly selected morning time periods each day. It is planned that the data from this baseline, if not autocorrelated, will be compared with the number of undesirable behaviors observed during random time frames each morning after a treatment has been initiated. Therefore, it is important first to determine whether these series of observations, obtained during the baseline period (the A phase), are independent of one another. If there is no correlation between the baseline behaviors, traditional forms of statistics can be used without violating their assumptions since there would be a fair level of certainty that the observations are independent. The numbers of baseline behaviors as they have been recorded over a period of 12 observations are:

6, 7, 8, 7, 8, 9, 10, 10, 9, 13, 9, 12

Procedural Steps for Calculating An Autocorrelation

It is advisable for the reader to follow the calculating steps found in Table 4-3 while reviewing these steps.

Table 4-3 Bartlett's Test (r_k)—Procedural Steps for Calculating an Autocorrelation

(STEP 1)

$$6 + 7 + 8 + 7 + 8 + 9 + 10 + 10 + 9 + 13 + 9 + 12 = 108$$

(STEP 2)

$$\frac{9.0}{12\overline{)108}} = \bar{X}$$

(STEP 3) Deviation Value	(STEP 4) Squared Deviation	(STEP 5) Multiplication of each deviation score by its succeeding deviation score and summing the resultant values
$(X - \bar{X})$	$(X - \bar{X})^2$	(1st dev. score) (2nd) + (2nd dev.) (3rd) + etc.
$6 - 9 = -3$	$(-3)^2 = 9$	$(-3)(-2) + (-2)(-1) +$
$7 - 9 = -2$	$(-2)^2 = 4$	$(-1)(-2) + (-2)(-1) +$
$8 - 9 = -1$	$(-1)^2 = 1$	$(-1)(\ 0) + (\ 0)(+1) +$
$7 - 9 = -2$	$(-2)^2 = 4$	$(+1)(+1) + (+1)(\ 0) +$
$8 - 9 = -1$	$(-1)^2 = 1$	$(\ 0)(+4) + (+4)(\ 0) +$
$9 - 9 = \ \ 0$	$(\ 0)^2 = 0$	$(\ 0)(+3) =$
		(further reduction follows below)
$10 - 9 = +1$	$(+1)^2 = 1$	$(+6) + (+2) +$
$10 - 9 = +1$	$(+1)^2 = 1$	$(+2) + (+2) +$
$9 - 9 = \ \ 0$	$(\ 0)^2 = 0$	$(\ 0) + (\ 0) +$
$13 - 9 = +4$	$(+4)^2 = 16$	$(+1) + (\ 0) +$
$9 - 9 = \ \ 0$	$(\ 0)^2 = 0$	$(\ 0) + (\ 0) +$
$12 - 9 = +3$	$(+3)^2 = \underline{9}$	$(\ 0) = 13$

Sum of $(X - \bar{X})^2 = 46$

STEP 6

$$r_k = \frac{13}{46} = .28$$

STEP 7

$$\frac{2}{\sqrt{n}} = \frac{2}{\sqrt{12}} = \frac{2}{3.46} = .58$$

STEP 8

$$B_r = \frac{r_k}{\dfrac{2}{\sqrt{n}}} = \frac{.28}{.58} = .48$$

1. The first step in the calculation of an autocorrelation is to sum the values listed above. Adding them gives a sum of 108.

2. Next, calculate the mean for the above distribution of numbers. Since the sum of the values is 108, and n (the number in the distribution) is 12, dividing 12 into 108 gives a mean ($\bar{X}$) of 9.0.

3. The third step is to subtract the mean from each score to establish a deviation value column.

4. The fourth step is to square each of the deviation values and sum the squared deviation values. The sum of the squared deviation values for this problem is 46.

5. The fifth step is to multiply each deviation value by its succeeding deviation value and then sum the multiplications which for this example adds to 13.

6. The sixth step is to divide the sum obtained in the fifth step, which was 13, by the sum of the squared deviation, which was 46. This is called Bartlett's test, symbolized as r_k, and the value of r_k for this example is equal to .28.

7. The seventh step is to divide 2 by the square root of n ($2/\sqrt{n}$) which equals .58.

8. The eighth and last step is to calculate Bartlett's ratio, also symbolized as B_r. The ratio is calculated by dividing the value obtained in Step 6 by the value obtained in Step 7. If the quotient is less than the absolute value of 1 ($|1|$), then the data are not autocorrelated. These data, therefore, have not been found to be autocorrelated because Bartlett's ratio (.28/.58 = .48) is less than $|1|$.

What has just been calculated is an *autocorrelation* of **lag 1** which was computed by pairing the initial observation with the second observation, the second observation with the third observation, etc. The correlation coefficient that was calculated is symbolized as r_1 representing a correlation of lag 1. Calculations for r_2, r_3, r_4, etc. could also be undertaken representing second, third, and fourth order correlations of the distribution. For most data in the behavioral sciences it is only necessary to calculate the first-order autocorrelation coefficient to see if the data are autocorrelated. Most of the time an autocorrelation of lag 1 suffices by providing information about whether the data are serially dependent. If more detailed analysis is desired then one goes on to obtain several autocorrelations with different "lag times." Usually

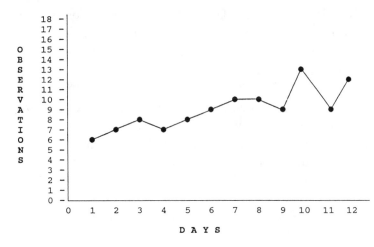

Figure 4-1 Plotted observations for baseline

these autocorrelations are performed by a computer. For example, a computer will calculate an autocorrelation of ''lag 2'' by comparing the first observation in a series with the third observation in that series, the second with the fourth, the third with the fifth, etc. The same procedure is also applicable to a lag of 3, but it is important to realize that the greater the spread between the lags the less accurate the results of the calculations will be because of a decrease in the number of pairs of observations that can be figured.

Before dealing with the treatment data obtained for the 12-year old acting out child, it might be a good idea first to see the plotted data for the baseline observations that have just been assessed and for which autocorrelation was not found.

The next data to be obtained would be information about the incidence of undesirable behaviors during the treatment or B phase of the study. Ten observations were made during 20-minute time intervals for one week while a behavior modification program was used to reduce undesirable behaviors. The treatment observations are shown below.

8, 5, 6, 2, 2, 6, 3, 5, 2, 1

Figure 4-2 shows a frequency polygon for both baseline and treatment data.

With only a few exceptions, if any statistical procedures are to be

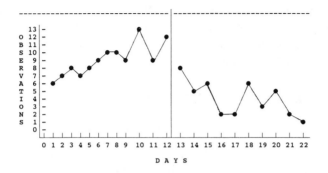

Figure 4-2 Plotted observations for both baseline
and treatment phases.

used, an autocorrelation must also be calculated for the treatment data
to make sure that these data are not serially related. Autocorrelations
must be computed separately within each phase and cannot be computed
across both phases. Calculating Bartlett's test for lag 1, to assess the
autocorrelation of observations during the treatment phase, yielded an
$r_k = .06$. Bartlett's ratio is $.06/.63 = .095$ which is less than $|1|$.
Therefore, the treatment data are not autocorrelated and it is already
known that the baseline data for lag 1 were not autocorrelated. Since
both sets of data appear to meet the independence of error assumption
we can now proceed to determine, using traditional statistics, whether
a significant difference exists between the baseline and treatment phases
of this study.

THE *T* TEST

One of several different types of statistics that could be used to
analyze the data that have just been assessed for autocorrelation is the
t test. The *t* test is a robust parametric statistic that will provide information as to whether a significant difference exists for two data sets.
The *t* test requires establishing a *null* (no difference) hypothesis. The
null hypothesis for this study is "there is no statistically significant
difference between the number of undesirable observed behaviors obtained during the baseline period as compared with the observations of
undesirable behaviors during the treatment phase." If the null hypothesis can be rejected then a significant difference has been found between

the baseline and treatment phases. If the null hypothesis cannot be rejected then no difference has been found between the two phases and the treatment would appear to have no statistically significant effect upon the child's behavior.

Procedural Steps for Calculating the *t* Test

Refer to Table 4-4 in following these procedural steps.

1. To begin calculation of a *t* test, the observations of undesirable behaviors for both the "A" (baseline) and "B" (treatment) phases should be established in tabular form as shown in Table 4-4. For the baseline data the symbol *X* will be used and the treatment data will use the symbol *Y*.

2. After the observed data has been listed, the squares for each value of *X* and *Y* should be calculated and placed into separate columns that have been labeled X^2 and Y^2 as shown in Table 4-4.

3. The next step is to sum each of the columns. The sum of the *X*, or baseline column, is 108, and the sum of the X^2 column is 1,018. The sum of the *Y*, or the treatment column, is 40 and the sum of Y^2 is 208. Under the *X* and *Y* columns in Table 4-4 the sum of *X* is depicted as $(\Sigma\ X)$ and the sum of *Y* $(\Sigma\ Y)$. Similarly the sum of X^2 is depicted as $(\Sigma\ X^2)$ and the sum of Y^2 is shown as $(\Sigma\ Y^2)$.

4. Then the value of *n* (number in the column) for each phase is determined. Since there were 12 baseline observations, the *n* for *X* is 12. The *n* for the treatment phase is 10. Looking at the numerator of the formula for the *t* test as found at the bottom of Table 4-4, note that the mean of *Y* must be subtracted from the mean of *X*. First, however, the means for both *X* and *Y* have to be calculated. The mean of *X* is found by dividing the sum of the observed behaviors which is 108 by the number of observations which is 12, yielding a mean of 9. Similarly the mean for *Y* is obtained by summing the behaviors in column *Y*, which are 40, and dividing the sum of the behaviors by the number in the column of 10 giving a mean of 4.

   Again referring to Table 4-4 at the means of *X* and *Y*, off to the right of the Table under the title "Combination," you will see a value of 5. That value was obtained by subtracting the mean of *Y* (which is 4) from the mean of *X* (which is 9). Thus, $\bar{X} - \bar{Y} = 5$, which is shown under the Combination column.

Table 4-4 Calculation of a t Test for both Baseline and Treatment Data.

Baseline data (A)		Treatment data (B)		
X	X^2	Y	Y^2	
6	36	8	64	
7	49	5	25	
8	64	6	36	
7	49	2	4	
8	64	2	4	
9	81	6	36	
10	100	3	9	
10	100	5	25	
9	181	2	4	
13	169	1	1	
9	181	40	208	
12	144			
108	1018			

$$\bar{X} = \frac{9}{12)\overline{108}} \qquad \bar{Y} = \frac{4}{10)\overline{40}} \qquad \text{Combination}$$

$\Sigma X = 108$	$\Sigma Y = 40$	
$n = 12$	$n = 10$	
$\bar{X} = 9$	$\bar{Y} = 4$	5
$(\Sigma X)^2 = 11{,}664$	$(\Sigma Y)^2 = 1600$	
$\dfrac{(\Sigma X)^2}{n} = \dfrac{11{,}664}{12} = 972$	$\dfrac{(\Sigma Y)^2}{n} = \dfrac{1600}{10} = 160$	
$\Sigma X^2 = 1{,}018$	$\Sigma Y^2 = 208$	
$SS_X = 46$ ____ + ____	$SS_Y = 48 \rightarrow$	94
$df_X = 11$ ____ + ____	$df_Y = 9 \rightarrow$	20
$S_C^2 =$		4.7
$\dfrac{1}{n_X} = \dfrac{1}{12} = .08$	$\dfrac{1}{n_Y} = \dfrac{1}{10} = .1$	.18

$$t = \frac{\bar{X} - \bar{Y}}{\sqrt{S_C^2 \left(\dfrac{1}{n_X} + \dfrac{1}{n_Y}\right)}} = \frac{9 - 4}{\sqrt{(4.7)\,.18}} = \frac{5}{\sqrt{.86}} = \frac{5}{.93} = 5.4$$

5. The next step is the calculation of the "Sum of Squares" represented by the symbol SS. The formula for the sum of squares for the baseline or X data is:

$$SS_x = \sum X^2 - \frac{(\sum X)^2}{n}$$

The formula for the sum of squares is exactly the same for the treatment or B phase except that instead of using Xs in the above formula, Ys are used.

Because two independent phases of data are being analyzed the sum of squares for both must be calculated and then combined. As seen in the above formula, the latter portion (the fraction) of the formula for the sum of squares consists of $(\sum X)^2/n$. That part will be considered first in the calculation of the sum of squares for the baseline behaviors. The sum of X the quantity squared, symbolized as $(\sum X)^2$, is obtained by multiplying the sum of X by itself. Thus, the sum of X is 108 and $(108)^2$ is 11,664. The formula then says to divide n into the $(\sum X)^2$. Since n is 12, the quotient obtained from dividing 11,664 by 12 is 972. The fractional portion of the sum of squares is now known to be 972. The first portion of the sum of squares formula is $\sum X^2$ (the sum of X square). This value has already been calculated by first squaring each of the X values and then summing those squared values. The sum of the squared X values is 1,018. Everything is now available for the baseline sum of squares formula, which would be calculated as follows

$$SS_x = \sum X^2 - \frac{(\sum X)^2}{n} = 1,018 - \frac{11,664}{12} = 1,018 - 972 = 46$$

The calculation for the sum of squares for the Y (treatment observations) would be:

$$SS_y = \sum Y^2 - \frac{(\sum Y)^2}{n} = 208 - \frac{1,600}{10} = 208 - 160 = 48$$

8. Once again looking at the "Combination" column in Table 4-4, across from the sums of squares (SS) for both the baseline and treatment phases, a value of 94 can be seen. That value was obtained by adding the sum of squares for the baseline (X) to the

sum of squares for the treatment (Y) phase. The SS for X is 46 and the SS for Y is 48. Adding both sums of squares together yields a combined sums of squares of 94 which is found in the combination column.

9. After calculating the combined sums of squares for both phases, the degrees of freedom must be determined. Degrees of freedom, symbolized as "df," are calculated by subtracting 1 from the number of observations in each phase. Since the baseline had 12 observations the degrees of freedom ($n - 1$) equals 11 for the baseline. Also, degrees of freedom of $n - 1$ are the same for the treatment phase so $10 - 1$ equals 9 degrees of freedom for B phase. The "Combination" column shows the sum of both the combined degrees of freedom for both phases or $11 + 9$ which is equal to 20 total degrees of freedom.

10. The formula for the t test at the bottom of Table 4-4 shows that the combined variance, symbolized as S_c^2, must be calculated and placed in the denominator under the square root sign. To calculate the combined variance the combined degrees of freedom, of 20, must be divided into the combined sums of squares, of 94. Therefore, carrying out the division yields a combined variance of 4.7.

11. The only thing left to do is calculate the values for $1/n_x$ and $1/n_y$ and that is easily done by dividing the number of observations found in the baseline period of 12 into 1 which is .08 and similarly dividing the number of observations during the treatment period of 10 divided into 1 yields a .1. Since the formula for the t test requires that these two values be summed together, the addition of both of the values is found in the combination column as .18.

12. Everything has now been completed for all values to be placed into the t test formula. The values are substituted into the formula as follows:

$$t = \frac{\overline{X} - \overline{Y}}{\sqrt{S_c^2 \left(\frac{1}{n_x} + \frac{1}{n_y} \right)}} = \frac{9 - 4}{\sqrt{(4.7)(.18)}} = \frac{5}{\sqrt{.86}} = \frac{5}{.93} = 5.4$$

The calculated t value for this problem is now known to be 5.4 and all the calculations are now completed.

13. All that remains to do is look up a value in Table 4-5 titled "Critical values of the *t* distribution." Before using the table of critical values for *t*, two things must be known.

First the level of significance must be selected. Traditionally levels of significance for the behavioral sciences are set at the .01 or the .05 levels of probability. Most clinical studies would probably use the .05 level and, therefore, Table 4-5 has been established only to provide critical values at the 5% level. The 5% level of significance simply means there is a 95% accuracy in *not* rejecting a true null hypothesis, but 5% of the time an error may be made by falsely rejecting a true null hypothesis. Statistical significance implies a change in data patterns or observations that would not be expected even if chance factors alone were operating to produce the results.

Second, the degrees of freedom must be known before the critical value can be identified in the *t* distribution table. The combined degrees of freedom have already been determined for this problem to be 20.

Table 4-5, which lists critical values of the *t* distribution, is read by going down the degrees of freedom column to 20 and across from the 20 to the value shown to the right under the column titled Critical Values. The intersect number which is called the **critical value** is 2.086. The calculated *t* value for the problem is then compared with the critical value found in the *t* distribution table. If the calculated value is larger than the critical value, the null hypothesis can be rejected. Since the calculated value is 5.4 and the critical value is 2.086 the null hypothesis can be rejected. It can now be said that a statistically significant difference has been found between the baseline and treatment observations to reduce undesirable behaviors. Since the null hypothesis can be rejected the research hypothesis is not rejected. The research hypothesis would be that the treatment was effective in reducing the number of undesirable behaviors found in this particular client.

Having concluded an explanation of the *t* test, another form of statistical analysis called the Mann-Whitney U (also known as the U test) will now be considered. The U test is a nonparametric procedure as compared to the just reviewed *t* test, which is a parametric statistic.

Parametric tests assume that data that are being used for analysis are

Table 4-5 Critical Values of the *t* Distribution
—Alpha Equals .05

df	Critical values
1	12.706
2	4.303
3	3.182
4	2.776
5	2.571
6	2.447
7	2.365
8	2.306
9	2.262
10	2.228
11	2.201
12	2.179
13	2.160
14	2.145
15	2.131
16	2.120
17	2.110
18	2.101
19	2.093
20	2.086
21	2.080
22	2.074
23	2.069
24	2.064
25	2.060
26	2.056
27	2.052
28	2.048
29	2.045
30	2.042
40	2.021
60	2.000
120	1.980
∞	1.960

*To reject the null hypothesis, the calculated *t* value must be greater than the critical *t* value found in this Table.

normally distributed or bell shaped. Nonparametric statistics make no such assumption. The nonparametric forms of statistics are, therefore, sometimes referred to as "distribution free" because they do not depend on the shape of the underlying distribution. While parametric methods, such as the t test make use of actual numerical observations, nonparametric methods do not use the actual scores or values in the statistical analysis. Instead they generally follow three procedures. They may require the ranking of the observed numerical scores, or they may use categorical information where observations are placed into categories or cells, or they may use plus or minus signs as a means for determining differences in scores between groups.

To repeat, the Mann-Whitney U is a nonparametric statistic which will be reviewed next as a method for analyzing single subject studies.

THE MANN-WHITNEY U TEST

It has previously been stated that with traditional statistics randomness of subjects is necessary to meet the assumptions allowing for generalization from a sample to a population. However, when there is only one subject it is obviously not possible to randomize that single individual nor is it possible to relate that person in a meaningful way to any population. The parametric t test that has just been reviewed shows that despite these limitations it is quite possible to use traditional statistics with data that are not serially related to determine whether a treatment has produced a statistically significant effect for a given person.

To consider the Mann-Whitney U test let us take an example of an attempt to assess the effectiveness of two different forms of treatment for a client who has Tourette's Syndrome. One major characteristic of this condition is an irresistible urge to shout obscenities. Thus, the ailment is often very disconcerting both to the individual as well as to those around that person.

A study was undertaken to determine which of two different treatment approaches would be more effective in reducing the profane outbursts of one particular individual. A psychiatrist and a skilled behavioral therapist provided two different treatments and a well trained observer recorded the number of obscene outbursts. One treatment involved the administration by the psychiatrist of Haldol, a neural depressant. The other used a behavior modification approach to change the client's actions. It was planned that each of the two treatments would be given seven times. A randomized procedure was used to determine during which session a particular treatment would be applied.

The "H" symbol in Table 4-6 represented the Haldol treatment and the "B" symbol the Behavioral treatment. A trained observer counted the number of obscene words that were uttered by the client during a 20-minute period immediately following each of the treatments. The data in Table 4-6 provides information on the order of the two different treatments as well as the number of verbal obscenities recorded after each treatment:

Table 4-7 shows the same data in tabular form.

The null hypothesis for this study was "there will be no difference in the number of obscene words used by the client during the observation periods following each of the treatment methods." Because the order of the treatments was randomized, the results would not favor one treatment over the other.

The Mann-Whitney U (also called the U test) was used to determine whether a significant difference existed for the data obtained from the two treatments as it is found in Table 4-7.

Table 4-6 Data Showing Number of Obscenities Following Each Treatment Session

H	B	B	H	B	H	H	B	H	B	B	H	H	B
7	6	7	9	7	8	8	6	10	9	5	12	7	5

Table 4-7 Number of Obscenities for Each Form of Treatment

Number of Obscenities Following Haldol Administration	Number of Obscenities Following Behavior Modification
7	6
9	7
8	7
8	6
10	9
12	5
7	5

Procedural Steps for Calculating the Mann-Whitney U

1. The first step requires the rank ordering of the combined values for both forms of treatment. The values have been ordered from the smallest, which is assigned the lowest rank, to the largest which received the highest rank, as seen in Table 4-8.

2. Next, after all the values have been ranked together they were then placed back into their original groups, as shown in Table 4-9. Each value for the first group, which was the "H" group, was then listed with its assigned rank. It was *not* necessary to do any calculations for the second or "B" group.

3. The ranks for the first group, the "H" group, were summed as shown in Table 4-9. The sum of the ranks is depicted as R_1. The numerical value is 70.5.

4. Next it was necessary to determine how many values were in each group. A quick count indicated that the first group, designated as n_1, had seven values as did the second group, shown as n_2, which also had seven values. Three values were now known: $n_1 = 7$, $n_2 = 7$, and sum of $R_1 = 70.5$. These three values were all that were necessary to solve for U by substituting the values using the following formula.

$$U = n_1 n_2 + \frac{n_1(n_2 + 1)}{2} - R$$

$$U = (7)(7) + \frac{7(7 + 1)}{2} - 70.5$$

Table 4-8 Ranked Values of Numbers of Obscenities

Combined Number of Obscenities for Both Treatment Groups	Absolute Rank Values	Averaged Rank Values
5	1	1.5
5	2	1.5
6	3	3.5
6	4	3.5
7	5	6.5
7	6	6.5
7	7	6.5
7	8	6.5
8	9	9.5
8	10	9.5
9	11	11.5
9	12	11.5
10	13	13.0
12	14	14.0

Table 4-9 Observed Values with Appropriate Ranks

Number of Obscenities Following Haldol Administration		Number of Obscenities Following Behavior Modification	
	Rank		Rank
7	6.5	6	3.5
9	11.5	7	6.5
$n_1 = 7$ 8	9.5	$n_2 = 7$ 7	6.5
8	9.5	6	3.5
10	13.0	9	11.5
12	14.0	5	1.5
7	6.5	5	1.5
Sum of R_1 = 70.5			

$$U = 49 + \frac{56}{2} - 70.5$$

$$U = 77 - 70.5 = 6.5$$

The observed or calculated U value is, therefore, **6.5**.

6. The next step was to look up the critical value for U which is found in Table 4-10. This Table provides critical values for U at the 5% level of significance. Note on Table 4-10 that the horizontal values listed across the top of the table are labeled n_S and those going down, along the left vertical margin, are labeled n_L. If different sized groups would have been studied, then the number of the smaller group symbolized as n_S would have been read along the top of the table and the number for the larger group would be read from the vertical left hand margin under the symbol n_L. The intersect value between the n_S and n_L values is called the **critical value**. Since both groups in our study each had an n of 7, the values for 7 were read on both axes without reference to either group because one group was neither larger nor smaller than the other. The intersect value of 7 on both axes is 8 which represents the **critical value** for this problem. The calculated U value must be equal to or less than the critical value or the null hypothesis cannot be rejected. Recall that the calculated U value was 6.5 and the critical value which has just been read from the Table of Critical Values for the Mann-Whitney U is 8. Since 6.5 is less than 8 these results indicate that given the two randomized treatments described above, there was a

Table 4-10 Critical Values for the Mann-Whitney U when Alpha is .05 on a Two-tailed Test

n_S

n_L	1	2	3	4	5	6	7	8	9	10	11	12	13	14	15	16	17	18	19	20
1	–	–	–	–	–	–	–	–	–	–	–	–	–	–	–	–	–	–	–	–
2	–	–	–	–	–	–	–	0	0	0	0	1	1	1	1	1	2	2	2	2
3	–	–	–	–	0	1	1	2	2	3	3	4	4	5	5	6	6	7	7	8
4	–	–	–	0	1	2	3	4	4	5	6	7	8	9	10	11	11	12	13	13
5	–	–	0	1	2	3	5	6	7	8	9	11	12	13	14	15	17	18	19	20
6	–	–	1	2	3	5	6	8	10	11	13	14	16	17	19	21	22	24	25	27
7	–	–	1	3	5	6	8	10	12	14	16	18	20	22	24	26	28	30	32	34
8	–	0	2	4	6	8	10	13	15	17	19	22	24	26	29	31	34	36	38	41
9	–	0	2	4	7	10	12	15	17	20	23	26	28	31	34	37	39	42	45	48
10	–	0	3	5	8	11	14	17	20	23	26	29	33	36	39	42	45	48	52	55
11	–	0	3	6	9	13	16	19	23	26	30	33	37	40	44	47	51	55	58	62
12	–	1	4	7	11	14	18	22	26	29	33	37	41	45	49	53	57	61	65	69
13	–	1	4	8	12	16	20	24	28	33	37	41	45	50	54	59	63	67	72	76
14	–	1	5	9	13	17	22	26	31	36	40	45	50	55	59	64	67	74	78	83
15	–	1	5	10	14	19	24	29	34	39	44	49	54	59	64	70	75	80	85	90
16	–	1	6	11	15	21	26	31	37	42	47	53	59	64	70	75	81	86	92	98
17	–	2	6	11	17	22	28	34	39	45	51	57	63	67	75	81	87	93	99	105
18	–	2	7	12	18	24	30	36	42	48	55	61	67	74	80	86	93	99	106	112

19	—	2	7	13	19	25	32	38	45	52	58	65	72	78	85	92	99	106	113	119
20	—	2	8	14	20	27	34	41	48	55	62	69	76	83	90	98	105	112	119	127
21	—	3	8	15	22	29	36	43	50	58	65	72	80	88	96	103	111	119	126	134
22	—	3	9	16	23	30	38	45	53	61	69	77	85	93	101	109	117	125	133	141
23	—	3	9	17	24	32	40	48	56	64	73	81	89	98	106	115	123	132	140	149
24	—	3	10	17	25	33	42	50	59	67	76	85	94	102	111	120	129	138	147	156
25	—	3	10	18	27	35	44	53	62	71	80	89	98	107	117	126	135	145	154	163
26	—	4	11	19	28	37	46	55	64	74	83	93	102	112	122	132	141	151	161	171
27	—	4	11	20	29	38	48	57	67	77	87	97	107	117	127	137	147	158	168	178
28	—	4	12	21	30	40	50	60	70	80	90	101	111	122	132	143	154	164	175	186
29	—	4	13	22	32	42	52	62	73	83	94	105	116	127	138	149	160	171	182	193
30	—	5	13	23	33	43	54	65	76	87	98	109	120	131	143	154	166	177	189	200
31	—	5	14	24	34	45	56	67	78	90	101	113	125	136	148	160	172	184	196	208
32	—	5	14	24	34	46	58	69	81	93	105	117	129	141	153	166	178	190	203	215
33	—	5	15	25	37	48	60	72	84	96	108	121	133	146	159	171	184	197	210	222
34	—	5	15	26	38	50	62	74	87	99	112	125	138	151	164	177	190	203	217	230
35	—	6	16	27	39	51	64	77	89	103	116	129	142	156	169	183	196	210	224	237
36	—	6	16	28	40	53	66	79	92	106	119	133	147	161	174	188	202	216	231	245
37	—	6	17	29	41	55	68	81	95	109	123	137	151	165	180	194	208	223	238	252
38	—	6	17	30	43	56	70	84	98	112	127	141	156	170	185	200	215	230	245	259
39	0	7	18	31	44	58	72	86	101	115	130	145	160	175	190	206	221	236	252	267
40	0	7	18	31	45	59	74	89	103	119	134	149	165	180	196	211	227	243	258	274

*To reject the null hypothesis, the calculated U value must be equal to or less than the critical value shown in the table. (Dashes indicate that no decision is possible.)

statistically significant difference in their effectiveness to control profane outbursts by a person with Tourette's Syndrome.

Scanning the data indicates that there were fewer obscenities following the behavior modification program than was true for the Haldol program.

Having completed this example a few comments need to be made. First, the Mann-Whitney U is an inferential nonparametric statistic which when used in a traditional way requires the presence of either a random sample from the population or random assignment of subjects to particular groups. Thus, it is usually used to make inferences about a population from a representative sample of that population. Rejecting a null hypothesis when the statistic is used for inferential analysis is quite different from the example shown here for a single subject. The hypothesis of the Mann-Whitney U with a single subject for whom two randomized treatments have been applied is that the treatments will not be different from each other in attaining a desired effect.

A weakness to keep in mind with this example is that one form of treatment may enhance the other treatment, but the reverse condition might not be the case. If one treatment, say *X*, did intensify the other treatment, called *Y*, then *Y* might possibly be found to be statistically significant from *X* even if *Y* was not really a more effective treatment.

Advantages and Disadvantages of the Mann-Whitney U

The Mann-Whitney U is a relatively easy statistic to calculate. A major advantage of this randomization test, when applied to single subject analysis, is that it does not have to rely on the same set of assumptions that are required for its use when employed for traditional inferential assessment. Also, serial dependency is not a problem when treatments have been randomly assigned, so concern about autocorrelation is unnecessary. In general the Mann-Whitney U or any other randomization tests should not be used if treatments produce irreversible behavior. In addition, there may be a problem created by the presentation of sequential treatments because of *carry-over* effects.

Another disadvantage of the U Test for statistical analysis, may be the impracticality of being able to implement random selection of individuals in a clinical setting. The condition of the clients may mitigate against a random procedure. Also it may not be possible to implement the random assignment of treatments to clients as, for example, when the client fails to show at the time when a particular intervention is to be given.

The next form of statistical analysis that will be discussed is called the R_n statistic. Developed by Revusky (1967) its primary use, the opposite of randomization tests, is when treatment effects are irreversible.

THE R_n STATISTIC

This statistic was first suggested by Revusky (1967) as a randomization method for analyzing conditions where treatment effects are irreversible and when a "multiple baseline design" has been employed. The procedure has enjoyed only limited acceptance in the research literature despite its several advantages, including simplicity of calculation. The R_n statistic analyzes data that have been simultaneously gathered on either two or more clients, a single client with two or more problems, or when two or more situations are used to treat the same problem. This statistic is helpful to the clinician because it essentially uses an A-B design. Withdrawal or reversal of treatment is not a necessary part of the research effort, as is the case with some of the other single subject designs.

The R_n test is more sensitive to nonchance results than either the nonparametric Mann-Whitney U or the parametric t test (Revusky, 1967). The focus of this statistic is on behavior changes resulting from a treatment or intervention. This test cannot assess statistical significance unless there are a minimum of a least four baseline observations.

When using the R_n test it is important to remember that whatever the focus of the multiple baseline, whether clients, problems, or situations, the intervention must be administered only once and in a random order.

An example applying the R_n statistic is illustrated across a multiple baseline design for a group of five culturally deprived children in a remedial mathematics class. The teacher decided to offer a reward of being able to watch cartoons as the method of intervention. The greater the improvement in the number of correct answers on mathematics exercises the longer the child was able to watch cartoons. Table 4-11 shows the data obtained for the five children.

Notice from Table 4-11 that the point of intervention, shown as a vertical line was begun after the fifth day. Notice also that after the

Table 4-11 Correctly Answered Mathematics Problems by Culturally Deprived Children in a Remedial Mathematics Class

	1	2	3	4	DAYS 5	6	7	8	9	10
Children										
John	20	23	21	18	30	25^a	27^b			
Jim	12	18	15	19	21	20^a	19^a	20^a	25^a	21^b
Harriet	31	30	25	29	33	29^a	33^a	37^b		
Jane	10	12	11	12	16	15^b				
Horace	29	35	37	35	40	39^a	41^a	43^a	49^b	

fifth day the children were randomly selected for administration of the treatment. For example, Jane was the first child who was selected at random to be given the treatment and her score of 15 is shown with the superscript "*b*." All of the other children were designated with the superscript "*a*" for the sixth day. The other children were still considered to be in a post-intervention baseline phase.

The second child to be randomly selected for treatment on the seventh day was John, whose score of 27 is also designated with a "*b*." Each day one child was randomly selected until only one child, Jim, remained for the tenth day and he was then given the treatment.

Procedural Steps for Calculating the R_n Statistic

After data has been entered into table form as shown in Table 4-11 the following steps should be used to calculate the R_n statistic.

1. First the mean of each child's scores, during the pre-intervention baseline should be calculated. For example, John's scores of 20, 23, 21, 18, and 30 sum to 112 and dividing 112 by the number of scores, which is 5, yields a mean for John's pre-intervention baseline scores of 22.4 which is placed under the mean value in Table 4-12. The mean score for every child should be calculated in the same way.

2. After the baseline means have been obtained the following formula is then applied.

$$PC_i = \frac{b - \bar{a}}{\bar{a}} \text{ where:}$$

PC_i: is the Percentage Change from the pre-intervention baseline mean score to the post-intervention treatment score for any one individual.

b: the post-intervention treatment score.

$\bar{a}$: the pre-intervention mean baseline score.

When one child receives a treatment intervention the raw scores on that day for all other children are also converted. For example, on the sixth day Jane was given a post-intervention treatment. Thus, in addition to converting Jane's score, all other children's post-intervention baseline scores must be computed. The mean for Jane's pre-intervention baseline scores is 12.2. Therefore, to convert to the "change percentage" the formula would be:

$$PC_i = \frac{b - \bar{a}}{\bar{a}} = \frac{15 - 12.2}{12.2} = \frac{2.8}{12.2} = .230$$

The .230, or 23% is the percentage change (increase) for Jane from the pre-intervention baseline mean to the post-intervention treatment. Having calculated the percentage of change for the one child who received the treatment then the "no treatment" post-intervention baseline scores for all other children for the same day are also calculated. For example, beginning with John, he had a post-intervention nontreatment baseline score of 25 and subtracting 22.4, his pre-intervention baseline mean, from 25 yields a remainder of 2.6. The 2.6 is then divided by 22.4, the mean for John's pre-intervention baseline scores, to obtain a quotient of .116. The .116 represents the percentage change (11.6% increase) that has occurred from the mean of the pre-intervention baseline for John. Table 4-12 shows all the percentage conversions for all the children in this multiple baseline study.

3. Once the change scores have been calculated for each individual in the post-intervention phase the next step is to rank the daily percentage changes for each child from high to low. To do the ranking it is important to remember whether the treatment was used to either increase or decrease the scores. If the intent was to increase the scores, as was the case with the present example where reward was

Table 4-12 Correctly Answered Mathematics Problems by Culturally Deprived Children in a Remedial Mathematics Class

Children	1	2	3	4	5	mean ($\bar{X}$)	6	7	8	9	10
John	20	23	21	18	30	(22.4)	25a (.116)	27b (.205)			
Jim	12	18	15	19	21	(17.0)	20a (.177)	19a (.118)	20a (.176)	25a (.47)	21b (.24)
Harriet	31	30	25	29	33	(29.6)	29a (.047)	33a (.115)	37b (.250)		
Jane	10	12	11	12	16	(12.2)	15b (.230)				
Horace	29	35	37	35	40	(35.2)	39a (.108)	41a (.165)	43a (.222)	49b (.392)	

based upon the child's correctly solving more mathematics problems, then the ranking would begin with the *highest* score (highest percent of change). The highest score would be given the value of 1 and all other lower scores would be ranked in ascending order. If, on the other hand, the intent of a study was to decrease the scores or values, then the ranking would assign the *lowest* score a rank of 1 and would rank in ascending order from the lowest to the highest score.

The ranking, therefore, for the study on improving mathematics scores is done for each day starting with the individual who had the highest percentage change. Table 4-13 shows the percentages of change in the post-intervention portion of the study. By adding the "*b*" treatment ranks shown in Table 4-13 for each day, the total sum of the ranks (ΣR) is obtained. On day 6, for example, the "*b*," or treatment rank was 1 and for day 7 it was 1, etc. Thus, $1 + 1 + 1 + 2 + 1 = 6$. Six represents the calculated value for R_n.

4. Next it is necessary to compare the Calculated Value of 6 with the Critical Values for R_n shown in Table 4-14. To read the table look down the column of N representing the number of individuals, problems, or situations in the study. For the present example there were 5 children so that N is equal to 5. Looking horizontally across from 5 representing the number for the study the critical value of 6 is seen at the intersect of $N = 5$ and the .05 level, or a critical value of 5 is seen at the intersect of $N = 5$ and the .01 level. In order to be able to state that a statistically significant change has occurred in these children the calculated R_n value must be equal to or smaller than the critical value found in Table 4-14. If the .01 alpha level had been selected prior to beginning the study the calculated value

Table 4-13 Display of Ranks for All Children

Day 6	Rank	Day 7	Rank	Day 8	Rank	Day 9	Rank	Day 10	Rank
.230 b	1	.205 b	1	.250 b	1	.470 a	1	.24 b	1
.177 a	2	.165 a	2	.222 a	2	.392 b	2		
.116 a	3	.118 a	3	.176 a	3				
.108 a	4	.115 a	4						
.047 a	5								

Percentage of Change for Each Day with "a" Representing Nontreatment During Post-Intervention and "b" Representing Treatment During the Post-Intervention Phase

Table 4-14 Critical Values of R_n for One-tailed Hypothesis

N	Level of Significance	
	.05	.01
4	4	
5	6	5
6	8	7
7	11	9
8	14	12
9	18	15
10	22	19
11	27	23
12	32	27
13	38	33
14	44	39

This table provides minimum values for rejection of the null hypothesis providing either the highest or lowest value is assigned a rank of 1 depending upon the predicted direction of treatment effects.

The calculated value of R_n must be equal to or less than the critical value found in this table in order to be able to reject the null hypothesis.

of R_n could not exceed the critical value of 5. Since the calculated value for this study was 6, it does exceed the critical value of 5, and a statistically significant improvement could not be claimed for the .01 level. However, at the .05 level the critical value is 6 and since 6 is equal to the calculated R_n value the null hypothesis that no change will occur can be rejected. Thus, this study found that by using a behavior modification technique the mathematics scores for these five children improved at the .05 level of significance.

Advantages and Disadvantages of the R_n Statistic

Generally multiple baseline designs carry out interventions for periods in excess of one treatment. The R_n statistic, however, uses only a single treatment for each individual to assess statistical significance. This one observation of the treatment's impact may be helpful for determining statistical significance, but it may not be meaningful to the practitioner in terms of clinical significance. The R_n statistic can be used when further evidence of change is desired if there is a clinical question about the effectiveness of the treatment.

As with other forms of randomization tests, the R_n statistic requires that individuals, situations, or behavioral problems should be randomly selected. Random selection in a clinical setting may be difficult to do. Sometimes staff are not ready or available to administer a particular treatment when the randomization process would call for it. Sometimes the client is not ready or available to receive the treatment. Also some clients must have immediate treatment while others may be able to tolerate delay, but unfortunately the client's needs cannot be primary if randomization is to be used. Thus, practical limitations may not realistically allow the carrying out of this type of analysis.

On the advantageous side, the R_n statistic is easy to calculate and will provide the practitioner with information about the effect of a given type of intervention. It must, however, be used with no less than four subjects, behaviors, or situations. Also the design used by the R_n statistic does not require the withdrawal of treatment as is the case with other types of single subject designs.

A significance of difference finding with the R_n does not mean that the treatment was effective for any one individual. It can only be said that the treatment was effective for the total of the individuals treated.

THE W STATISTIC

Revusky's R_n statistic, which has just been reviewed, was one of the first randomization tests to be proposed for multiple baseline, single subject, research. His method requires that treatment be terminated for each subject (behavior or situation) immediately after its administration. If the research-practitioner, using a multiple baseline design, wishes to continue beyond one treatment phase the R_n statistic cannot be used. Another form of analysis, called the W statistic (Wampold and Worsham, 1986), is an alternative approach to determine whether a treatment has had a statistically significant effect. The W statistic is based upon the works of Fisher (1951) and Edgington (1980). Fisher first suggested the idea of a test based upon permutations of the observations in his discussion of Galton's analysis of an experiment by Darwin. Fisher was concerned with the development of a system that would measure the height of plants based upon a random selection of 15 pairs of seeds.

The W statistic is one of several randomization methodologies that can be used when treatment is applied to subjects (behaviors or situations) in a multiple baseline design. An advantage of the randomization test is that no assumption of random sampling is required, but a negative consequence is that inference of results is restricted to only those individuals who were sampled for a study. This procedure, as well as other randomization tests, is based upon the assumption that the observations of an experiment are equally likely to be associated with any treatment. The permutations of the observations are then considered to be equally likely outcomes of the research.

The W statistic does not require that the treatment of choice be stopped after each intervention as is the case with R_n. Instead, the W statistic compares the baseline for each person to the treatment phase for that individual rather than to untreated phases as is the case with R_n.

As explained in Chapter 2, the multiple baseline design introduces a treatment at different points in time, thus helping to control for history as a threat to internal validity (Harris and Jensen, 1985). Usually the multiple baseline design is replicated for two, three or four subjects (behaviors or situations) and the W statistic is well suited for this type of design because it enables the reseacher to analyze the treatments of each. The W statistic uses randomization as a procedure for selecting the order in which the subjects, behaviors, or situations receive a treatment. There is no need to be concerned about autocorrelation of the data when using the W statistic.

Subjects, rather than behaviors or situations, will be used to explain the randomization process and the application of the W statistic. Randomization, however, is just as applicable to behaviors or situations.

A researcher working with two individuals, say Alice and Ben, would have two possible random orders of selection for these two people. Either Alice could come first and she could be designated as A_1 and Ben would come second, with the designation B_2 (A_1, B_2), or Ben could come first designated as B_1 and Alice could come second as A_2 (B_1, A_2). If there were three individuals, Alice (A), Ben (B) and Curtis (C), there would be six possible orders of selection. They would be: A_1 B_2 C_3, A_1 C_2 B_3, B_1 A_2 C_3, B_1 C_2 A_3, C_1 A_2 B_3, and C_1, B_2, A_3. Without subscripts these arrangements could also be written as ABC, ACB, BAC, BCA, CAB and CBA. What has just been described is a **permutation**.

Often in research we want to know how many different ways a set of people, behaviors or situations can be arranged. In the example where there were only two people, Alice and Ben, two different arrangements were possible without duplication. This means that if two spaces have been allocated there are only two ways that the two individuals can be arranged to fill those two spaces without duplication. If the spaces are depicted as 1 and 2, the first position might be occupied by A being first and B being second, but once that arrangement has been used it cannot be used again. Therefore, the second space could only be established by showing B being first and A coming second. Thus, the first space could be *A,B* and the second space would be *B,A*, or the reverse arrangement could also be the case. When there are only two people the symbol for the permutation, the total number of unduplicated arrangements, is represented as 2! (read as two factorial) where each number on the left starting with 2 is multiplied by its succeeding next lower number on the right. Thus, $2 \times 1 = 2$. Two unduplicated arrangements, therefore, are the limit for two people. If there are three individuals the permutation is symbolized as 3!, which would be $3 \times 2 \times 1 = 6$. Three factorial has a maximum of six possible unduplicated arrangements. The permutation for four individuals is symbolized as 4! or $4 \times 3 \times 2 \times 1 = 24$. Thus, 24 represents the total number of ways that four people could be arranged. Five individuals (5!) would permute to 120 and 6 (6!) to 720.

The W statistic is computed based upon the permutation of all individuals, behaviors, or situations, in a particular multiple baseline study. Refer to Table 4-14A and note there are four individuals—Alice, Ben, Curtis and Daisy, all of whom are moderately retarded diurnally enuretic children. A treatment to reduce wetting consisted of praise each time a check showed dry pants. Each child was examined once an hour over a twenty five day period and the number of accidents were recorded. Since there were four children (4!), there are 24 possible

Table 4-14A Examinations Over a 25-Day Period When a Child Had Wet Pants

	Block 1	Block 2	Block 3	Block 4	Block 5
Alice	4 2 5 4 2	4 5 4 3 3	4 1 3 2 3	4 3 2 1 1	0 2 2 1 0
Ben	5 6 7 6 4	6 5 7 5 4	3 3 3 2 1	4 2 3 2 5	2 1 2 0 1
Curtis	4 4 3 5 3	4 5 6 3 4	5 4 1 2 1	3 0 0 1 2	2 1 0 1 0
Daisy	7 5 6 6 7	4 6 7 6 5	6 7 4 5 7	7 5 3 3 4	2 1 3 2 1

combinations of individuals, which are: ABCD, ABDC, ACBD, ACDB, ADBC, ADCB, BACD, BADC, BCAD, BCDA, BDAC, BDCA, CADB, CABD, CBAD, CBDA, CDAB, CDBA, DABC, DACB, DBAC, DBCA, DCAB, DCBA.

The W statistic by Wampold and Worsham (1986) is based upon the sum across the subjects of the difference in means between baseline and treatment phases. The above permutation depicts a distribution of all 24 possible arrangements of these individuals that could be used for their treatment in a multiple baseline study.

Each permutation is assigned a number and 1 out of the 24 permutations listed above is then selected randomly either by a table of random numbers or by any other random selection procedure such as drawing numbers out of the familiar fishbowl. The one permutation that is randomly selected is then used to conduct the study. The randomly selected permutation for this study was BACD. Selecting BACD meant that the study was based upon Ben being given the first treatment, Alice the second, Curtis the third, and Daisy the last intervention. No other permutations were given a treatment and W for each permutation was calculated from the data on each subject as seen in Table 4-14B.

The assumption of the W statistic is that if the treatment has a sufficient effect size, which is the same as saying that it produces beneficial change, the value of W for the one permutation selected for treatment will be larger than all other permutations for the individuals in the study.

Notice in Table 4-14A there were five observations for each block in this study. The use of five observations is based upon the decision to use a baseline consisting of five observations which provided the basis for calculations of all baseline and treatment phases. Blocks for other studies, based upon the number of the first baseline observations, might consist of different numbers of observations, such as three or four or six. Because the first baseline for this study consisted of five observations, additional blocks, either baseline or treatment phases for the first individual and all other individuals in the study, also contain five observations each. Table 4-14A provides data about the number of times that wet pants were observed each time a particular child was examined.

Having obtained the data found in Table 4-14A for each of these children it is now possible to construct Table 4-14B. Table 4-14B shows the baseline and treatment phases for all of the possible permutations for each child and allows for the calculation of the W statistic.

Table 4-14B Randomization Arrangements for Four Children

	$\bar{A}_1 - \bar{B}_1$	$\bar{A}_2 - \bar{B}_2$	$\bar{A}_3 - \bar{B}_3$	$\bar{A}_4 - \bar{B}_4$	W
ABCD	3.4 — 2.40(1.00)	5.5 — 2.27(3.23)	3.60 — 1.0(2.60)	5.50 — 1.8(3.70)	10.53
ABDC	3.4 — 2.40(1.00)	5.5 — 2.27(3.23)	5.87 — 3.1(2.77)	3.00 — 0.8(2.20)	9.20
ACBD	3.4 — 2.40(1.00)	4.1 — 1.53(2.57)	4.47 — 2.2(2.27)	5.50 — 1.8(3.70)	9.54
ACDB	3.4 — 2.40(1.00)	4.1 — 1.53(2.57)	5.87 — 3.1(2.77)	4.15 — 1.2(2.95)	9.29
ADBC	3.4 — 2.40(1.00)	5.9 — 4.00(1.90)	4.47 — 2.2(2.27)	3.00 — 0.8(2.20)	7.37
ADCB	3.4 — 2.40(1.00)	5.9 — 4.00(1.90)	3.60 — 1.0(2.60)	4.15 — 1.2(2.95)	8.45
BACD	5.6 — 3.05(2.55)	3.6 — 1.93(1.67)	3.60 — 1.0(2.60)	5.50 — 1.8(3.70)	10.52
BADC	5.6 — 3.05(2.55)	3.6 — 1.93(1.67)	5.87 — 3.1(2.77)	3.00 — 0.8(2.20)	9.19
BCAD	5.6 — 3.05(2.55)	4.1 — 1.53(2.57)	3.27 — 1.6(1.67)	5.50 — 1.8(3.70)	10.49
BCDA	5.6 — 3.05(2.55)	4.1 — 1.53(2.57)	5.87 — 3.1(2.77)	3.00 — 1.0(2.00)	9.89
BDAC	5.6 — 3.05(2.55)	5.9 — 4.00(1.90)	3.27 — 1.6(1.67)	3.00 — 0.8(2.20)	8.32
BDCA	5.6 — 3.05(2.55)	5.9 — 4.00(1.90)	3.60 — 1.0(2.60)	3.00 — 1.0(2.00)	9.05
CABD	3.8 — 2.25(1.55)	3.6 — 1.93(1.67)	5.87 — 3.1(2.77)	4.15 — 1.2(2.95)	8.94
CADB	3.8 — 2.25(1.55)	3.6 — 1.93(1.67)	4.47 — 2.2(2.27)	5.50 — 1.8(3.70)	9.19
CBAD	3.8 — 2.25(1.55)	5.5 — 2.27(3.23)	3.27 — 1.6(1.67)	5.50 — 1.8(3.70)	10.15
CBDA	3.8 — 2.25(1.55)	5.5 — 2.27(3.23)	5.87 — 3.1(2.77)	3.00 — 1.0(2.00)	9.55
CDAB	3.8 — 2.25(1.55)	5.9 — 4.00(1.90)	3.27 — 1.6(1.67)	4.15 — 1.2(2.95)	8.07
CDBA	3.8 — 2.25(1.55)	5.9 — 4.00(1.90)	4.47 — 2.2(2.27)	3.00 — 1.0(2.00)	7.72
DABC	6.2 — 4.40(1.80)	3.6 — 1.93(1.67)	4.47 — 2.2(2.27)	3.00 — 0.8(2.20)	7.94
DACB	6.2 — 4.40(1.80)	3.6 — 1.93(1.67)	3.60 — 1.0(2.60)	4.15 — 1.2(2.95)	9.02
DBAC	6.2 — 4.40(1.80)	5.5 — 2.27(3.23)	3.27 — 1.6(1.67)	3.00 — 0.8(2.20)	8.90
DBCA	6.2 — 4.40(1.80)	5.5 — 2.27(3.23)	3.60 — 1.0(2.60)	3.00 — 1.0(2.00)	9.63
DCAB	6.2 — 4.40(1.80)	4.1 — 1.53(2.57)	3.27 — 1.6(1.67)	4.15 — 1.2(2.95)	8.99
DCBA	6.2 — 4.40(1.80)	4.1 — 1.53(2.57)	4.47 — 2.2(2.27)	3.00 — 1.0(2.00)	8.64

Procedural Steps for Calculating the W Statistic

The following steps can be used to calculate the W statistic.

1. The first permutation shown in Table 4-14B is ABCD. The initial baseline data for Alice, the first individual in this permutation, is calculated based upon the block of the first five data points which are: 4, 2, 5, 4, and 2. The sum of these values is 17 and the mean of 3.4 for the baseline was obtained by dividing 17 by the number of data points which are five. Then beyond Alice's baseline data are four blocks or 20 treatment observations. They were: 4, 5, 4, 3, 3, | 4, 1, 3, 2, 3, | 4, 3, 2, 1, 1, | 0, 2, 2, 1, 0. These observations sum to 48 and the mean for Alice's treatment observations were calculated by dividing the sum of the treatment observations by the number (n) of treatment observations. Thus, 20 into 48, yields a mean for Alice's treatment observations of 2.4. Note in Table 4-14B that the mean of the first baseline for Alice in the ABCD permutation is shown under $\overline{A}_1$ as 3.4 and the mean for her treatment observations is shown under $\overline{B}_1$ as 2.4. The difference was obtained between Alice's baseline and treatment means, when she was in the first position, by subtracting the mean of the treatments, which was 2.4, from the mean of the baseline which was 3.4. The remainder is shown in parenthesis next to the values for $\overline{A}_1$ and $\overline{B}_1$ as a value of 1.00.

2. Ben was the second person in this permutation and his baseline data was calculated as if the treatment had been implemented after Ben's second block of data points. Thus, Ben's baseline data for the first permutation would be his beginning two blocks of data or the first 10 values. These were: 5, 6, 7, 6, 4, | 6, 5, 7, 5, 4 which sum to 55. The mean of the baseline data for Ben in this permutation is obtained by dividing 55 by 10 which is the total number of baseline points, yielding a quotient of 5.5. The mean of 5.5 is seen in Table 4-14B under $\overline{A}_2$. Once Ben's baseline mean had been calculated then his treatment mean, for the permutation of ABCD was determined. Since two blocks or 10 data points were used for Ben's baseline his treatment is considered to begin after the second block or at the first observation of the third block. This means there are three remaining blocks or 15 observations. These values are: 3, 3, 3, 2, 1, | 4, 2, 3, 2, 5, | 2, 1, 2, 0, 1 and they sum to 34. Then dividing 34 by 15, the number of observations during Ben's treatment for this permutation, provides a mean of 2.27. Subtracting 2.27 from

5.5 gives a remainder of 3.23 which is shown in parenthesis under the column labeled $\overline{A}_2 - \overline{B}_2$.

3. Curtis's data, since he was third in the ABCD permutation, was the third baseline to be considered. The third baseline is considered to be 3 blocks or 15 observations. The 15 observations are: 4, 4, 3, 5, 3, | 4, 5, 6, 3, 4, | 5, 4, 1, 2, 1. The sum of these 15 observations is 54. The mean for Curtis's baseline of three blocks or 15 observations was obtained by dividing 54 by 15 which yields a quotient of 3.6. The value 3.6 is shown under $\overline{A}_3$ for the ABCD permutation. Next the mean for Curtis's treatment phases was calculated. There were two remaining blocks or 10 treatment observations in this permutation for Curtis and these were: 3, 0, 0, 1, 2, | 2, 1, 0, 1, 0. The mean for this treatment data is 1 based upon the sum of the observations which was 10 and this sum being divided by the number of observations of 10.

Therefore, $\overline{B}_3$ for the first permutation is 1. The difference between baseline and treatment means for Curtis was 3.6 minus 1 or 2.6, which is shown in parenthesis.

4. The last child in this permutation was Daisy. As she was the fourth child, her baseline extends for four blocks or 20 observations. These were:

7, 5, 6, 6, 7, | 4, 6, 7, 6, 5, | 6, 7, 4, 5, 7, | 7, 5, 3, 3, 4.

The mean for these observations is calculated in the same manner as shown previously by dividing the sum of the observations by n, yielding a quotient of 5.5. That value can be seen under $\overline{A}_4$. Since Daisy was the fourth subject there are only five treatment observations for her, which is the fifth block consisting of the values: 2, 1, 3, 2, 1. These numbers sum to 9 which when divided by n, or five, for the number of observations in the treatment block yields a mean treatment of 1.8 which is shown under $\overline{B}_4$. Subtracting Daisy's mean treatment phase from her baseline phase provides a remainder of 3.7 which is seen in parenthesis under the values for $\overline{A}_4 - \overline{B}_4$ for the permutation ABCD. Once the treatment means have been subtracted from the baseline means for the four subjects in the ABCD permutation all values in the parentheses for that permutation are then summed. The sum of 1, 3.23, 2.6, and 3.7 is 10.53 which is the W value for the ABCD permutation.

The next permutation in Table 4-14B is ABDC. This permutation is calculated in the same manner as the procedure that has just been reviewed. An explanation for the calculation of W for the second permutation may help to clarify any questions that still remain.

1. The permutation following ABCD is ABDC. The arrangement of children in this permutation shows that Alice was first, Ben was second, Daisy was third and Curtis was fourth. Thus, Alice's baseline would be calculated for the first block of five observations. The next 20 observations would be the treatment phase. The mean for Alice's baseline phase is 3.4 and for her treatment the mean is 2.4. The value in the parenthesis for the ABDC permutation indicating the difference between Alice's first baseline and her treatment phases is 1, as shown under the column $\overline{A}_1 - \overline{B}_1$.

2. Since Ben came next, as the second subject in this permutation, his baseline consisted of the first and second blocks or ten observations. Adding the first 10 observations for Ben and dividing those observations by the baseline n of 10 yields a mean of 5.5. Since two blocks were used for Ben's baseline, because he was second in the permutation of ABCD, then Ben's remaining three treatment blocks must be summed and divided by treatment n, or 15, to obtain the mean for Ben's treatment phase for permutation ABDC. The treatment mean was calculated to be 2.27 and the difference as shown in parenthesis under column $\overline{A}_2 - \overline{B}_2$ is 3.23.

3. Next is Daisy. She is in the third position in this permutation and, therefore, her baseline is calculated through three blocks or 15 observations. Daisy's remaining 10 observations beyond her baseline are her treatment phase and the difference for means between Daisy's baseline and treatment phases is determined and shown in the parenthesis under $\overline{A}_3 - \overline{B}_3$.

4. The last individual, in the fourth position for this permutation, is Curtis. Since he is in the fourth position his baseline is extended through four blocks or 20 observations and his treatment consists of the balance of his data or one block of treatment observations.

5. W for each successive permutation has been calculated by similarly rearranging the data.

Significance of the Treatment Based Upon the *W* Statistic

If the treatment in this study had been beneficial for these four subjects than the largest value for W would be for that permutation where the subjects actually received the treatment. Looking at Table 4-14B it can be seen that the largest W did not occur where treatment was implemented in permutation BACD. The W value for that permutation was 10.52. The largest W value in Table 4-14B was 10.53, which was for the ABCD permutation.

The question remains as to the statistical significance of these findings. The alpha level, the probability of making an error by rejecting a true null hypothesis, is obtained by dividing the number of permutation values in the distribution that were as large or larger than the treatment permutation by the total number of permutations. Because, the largest W value was the ABCD permutation and the second largest value was the BACD permutation which was the treatment permutation, a value of 2 permutations is obtained. When 2 is divided by the number of permutations in the distribution the alpha level is obtained. Thus 2 divided by 24 yields a quotient of .083. Assuming that .05 is an acceptable alpha level, the null hypothesis that "no treatment effect could be detected" can not be rejected because .083 is larger than .05. Therefore, the null hypothesis that the treatment had no effect could not be rejected. The conclusion is that "the treatment had no statistically significant effect." If the treatment permutation would have been the highest value then that one permutation would have been divided by 24 yielding an alpha value of .042, which is an acceptable alpha level for rejection of the null hypothesis.

It is quite obvious that when there are only four individuals who are permuted, the only time that a significant treatment effect can be detected, using the W statistic, is when the treatment produces the permutation with the highest value. If any other permutation results in a W value that is higher than the treatment permutation no significance of treatment can be claimed because the null hypothesis cannot be rejected at an accepable alpha level.

Thus, requiring the treatment permutation to have the highest W value in order to reject the null hypothesis provides minimal opportunity for rejection of the null hypothesis when using the W statistic for four subjects. If, however, five subjects are used the permutation of 5! results in a randomized distribution consisting of 120 permutations. This is obtained by multiplying $5 \times 4 \times 3 \times 2 \times 1 = 120$. With this number of permutations an alpha level that is less than .01 can be obtained and as many as five W's could be larger than the treatment W while still allowing for rejection of the null hypothesis at the .05 level of significance. Therefore, as the number of subject (behaviors or situations) increase an acceptable alpha level can be obtained, but simultaneously the number of permutations become overwhelming to create by hand.

Probably the best method of solving the arduous task of calculating W values for so many permutations, aside from employing computer analysis, is to use a random sampling process suggested by Barnard (1963). Instead of using all possible permutations of the observations for computing the level of probability to be able to reject the null hypothesis, a random sample is generated and taken to represent the whole set of permutations. As an example, if there are seven subjects, 7! would equal 5,040. Hand calculating W's for this number of permuations would certainly be unreasonable. However, there is an acceptable way to reduce the total number of computations for this statistic. First, all of the permutations for the seven subjects would have to be calculated. These permutations would have to be derived by means of a computer program described, for example, by Edgington (1987). Once all permutations had been determined a sample from the 5,040 possible permutations could be selected by using a Table of Random Numbers. The treatment permutation would be randomly assigned to one of the sample of permutations and the previously described procedure could then be followed to calculate the W values for the reduced number of permutations. The sampled permutations, while still requiring a number of calculations, would permit for rejection of the null hypothesis at the .01 level.

Advantages and Disadvantages of the W Statistic

The W statistic, as one form of randomization test, is a valid method for single subject statistical analysis. Randomization tests by themselves, in the strict sense of the word, are not statistical tests. Rather, they are used to determine the significance level of a particular statistical test. As long as the randomization process is followed without violations, the level of significance is well-grounded. A randomization procedure, based upon independence of observations between baseline and treatment phases, is generally credible for any analysis because it eliminates the problem of autocorrelation by permuting all of the data in the distribution.

The W statistic is similar to Revusky's R_n in that it uses a random selection procedure to introduce the treatment. It is different from the R_n because it compares a continuing baseline phase with subjects (behaviors or situations) that have not received the treatment. R_n is more applicable for research where measurement is terminated immediately or shortly after the treatment has been introduced. The W statistic allows the researcher to continue measuring the treatment effects for all elements before treatment is discontinued. By virtue of this capability the W statistic more closely approximates procedures commonly employed by single subject researchers who usually try to compare the baseline of one element, e.g., a subject, with that individual's treatment phase, rather than with an untreated phase. The use of the W statistic in a clinical setting should not impose a hardship on either the researcher or the clients since the randomization process can be carried out without effecting the clients themselves.

Usually when the clinical researcher plans to use the W statistic, data will be collected based upon the randomly selected permutation. While it is traditionally considered to be a violation of statistical procedures to select the manner of statistical analysis before the data is collected, there does not appear to be a problem connected with an a priori selection in this instance. The randomization process and the use of the W statistic is no different from most other single subject research which generally involves selection of a statistic before the collection of data.

THE CELERATION LINE METHOD FOR EVALUATING BEHAVIORAL CHANGE

Another technique has been developed that uses a trend line to assess the nature of behavioral change in a single subject. There are two versions of the trend line approach. The first has been called the **split-middle** (Kazdin, 1976, White, 1972, 1974) and the second the **celeration line** (Bloom & Fischer, 1982). The split middle method uses median scores to calculate a trend line that is adjusted, either up or down, to ensure that half of the scores being evaluated in the first phase are above and half are below the line. The celeration line is based upon two mean scores representing the first and second halves of the baseline data and the line is not adjusted. Since both methods are very similar, except for some minor computational differences, the celeration line has been selected for review.

Use of the celeration line requires the careful plotting of both baseline and treatment data on a graph. The intent is to use the first phase, usually the baseline data, to develop a trend line that will predict the extent of the change in behavior during the treatment period.

The term "celeration line" is derived from the concepts of acceleration and deceleration, that is, increasing or decreasing rates of change. The celeration line method of evaluating client behavior is based upon what is called the binomial distribution. This method is used to determine whether a trend observed in one phase, the baseline period, will continue through a following phase, the treatment period.

The assertion has been made that the celeration line method does not require independence of data and, therefore, may be especially useful for data that are autocorrelated (Bloom and Fischer, 1982). One of the basic assumptions for using a binomial test, however, assumes that any data are unaffected by previous data. Thus, the assumptions of a binomial test, which the celeration line is based on, are violated when used with autocorrelated data (Crosbie, 1987). Since the binomial clearly requires independent data, and because the celeration line is based on the binomial distribution, an assessment should be made to determine whether autocorrelation is present before the celeration line technique is used.

When using the celeration line it is recommended that no fewer than 10 observations be used for the baseline and no less than five for the treatment phase. These minimum numbers of observations during each phase will provide a sufficiently accurate fitting of the celeration line to avoid drawing erroneous conclusions. Fewer observations during each phase will compromise the procedure resulting in statistical decision errors. More than the minimum number of observations poses no problem.

Procedural Steps for Calculating a Celeration Line

The following steps can be used to calculate a celeration line. Refer to Figure 4-3 and Figure 4-4 as these steps are discussed.

1. Baseline data, which is typically the first phase (A) of most single subject designs, are gathered. The intent is to compare the client's behavioral baseline data with the targeted behavior that will be gathered during the treatment phase. Once the baseline data have been obtained it is plotted on a frequency polygon showing the frequency of behaviors by means of a line. Planning the size of the values on both the ordinate (the vertical axis) and abscissa (the horizontal axis) of the graph will depend on the expected range of the behaviors

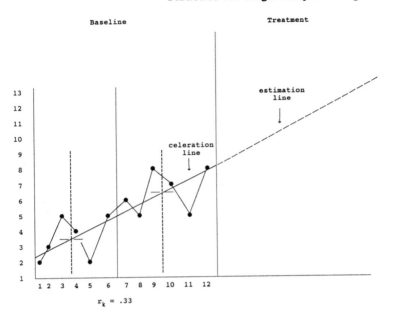

Figure 4-3 Celeration and estimation lines

and the number of observation sessions. For example, if the number of behaviors observed are expected to be as many as 50, then the graph should be numbered up to 50. Observations of the client's behavior should be numbered up the ordinate and the sessions (e.g., the times of the observations in hours, days, weeks, etc.) should be numbered along the abscissa. Graphing a celeration line without using graph paper should not be attempted because errors in drawing the line can seriously affect the accuracy of the results.

2. The baseline period is sectioned into two equal parts determined by the total number of baseline observations. Figure 4-3 shows the baseline being divided by a solid vertical line immediately after the sixth day because the total baseline phase was for 12 days. If the number of baseline observations is odd, then a solid vertical line is drawn through the middle observation. Since, in this example, each half of the baseline period had an even number of 6 days, the dotted vertical line is drawn immediately after the third day for the first half of the baseline and immediately after the ninth day for the second half of the baseline.

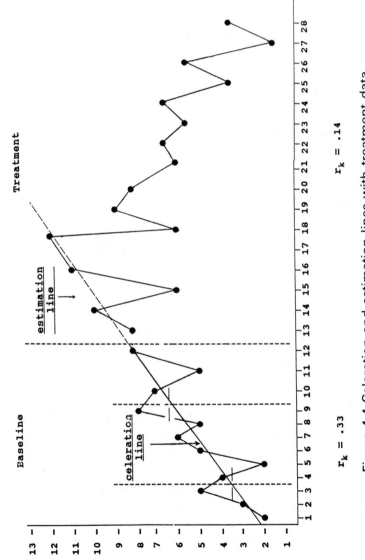

Figure 4-4 Celeration and estimation lines with treatment data

3. A mean ($\overline{X}$) must then be calculated for each of the baseline halves. This is accomplished by adding all of the values in the first half-baseline and dividing by the total number in that half-baseline period. Referring to Figure 4-3 there are six plotted points in the first half-baseline representing half of the total baseline observations. The sum of the values 2, 3, 5, 4, 2, 5 which are found in the first half of the baseline is 21 and dividing the sum of the values (21) by n, which is 6, gives a mean of 3.5 for that half. Note on the first dotted vertical line, splitting the first half of the baseline, a short horizontal slash mark has been placed on it at the plotted value of 3.5. The same procedure is then followed for the second half of the baseline. The second half has the values 6, 5, 8, 7, 5, 8. The sum of these values is 39 and 39 divided by n, which again is 6, gives a mean ($\overline{X}$) for the second half of the baseline of 6.5. The second vertical line is shown with a short horizontal slash mark at the plotted value of 6.5.

4. There are now two dotted vertical lines, representing the first and third quartile of the baseline distribution that have short horizontal slash marks. A straight solid line should be drawn through the intersecting values where the slash marks are located, that is between 3.5 and 6.5. This straight solid line should be changed to a dashed line as it continues past the baseline into the treatment phase of the graph. The straight solid line that was drawn through the two slash marks of the baseline phase is called a **celeration line**. The line with dashes, representing the portion that extends from the celeration line through the treatment phase, is called the **estimation line**. Note in Figure 4-3 that the celeration line is accelerating during the baseline phase and the estimation line follows the celeration line in an accelerating direction. If the celeration line was decelerating it would be going in a downward direction—the opposite of what is seen in Figure 4-3.

5. Next a decision must be made by the research-practitioner about whether the treatment goal is to increase or decrease client behaviors. If the goal is to produce increased behaviors over the baseline, the hypothesis is that more of the behaviors would fall above the estimation line. For example, if the treatment goal was to produce increased weight for an anorectic client then it would be assumed that the result in weight or food intake values would be above the "estimation line." If they did not fall above the estimation line the

treatment results would be questionable. On the other hand there are times when a clinician may be treating a client where the goal is to reduce a particular form of behavior. For example, if a child is treated to reduce thumb sucking, the clinician's goal would be to reduce the amount of time (or perhaps the number of times) that the child would spend in thumb sucking. In this instance the goal would be for the behavior to be reduced and to fall below the "estimation line." If the treatment data did not fall below the "estimation line" the clinician would probably feel that the intervention was ineffective.

The question, however, for each of the above examples is, "how many of the increased eating behaviors above the line are needed to conclude that the treatment was "really" effective. Similarly, for the second example, how much reduction of thumb sucking would support the hypothesis that the treatment was "really" effective? It is in answer to such questions that the celeration line technique becomes useful.

6. The next step, to ascertain whether a treatment has produced a significant change, is begun by counting the total number of observations that were made during the baseline phase. Looking at Figure 4-4 there are 12 plotted points in the baseline phase. Next, count how many behaviors fall either above or below the celeration line. Whether the count is made of observations falling above or below the line depends upon the hypothesized goal of the treatment. If the treatment goal was to increase the targeted behaviors, then the plotted points that fall *above* the celeration line should be counted. If the treatment goal was to decrease behavior, then the number of plotted points *below* the celeration line would be counted.

Figure 4-4 presents a graph depicting the treatment efforts of a research-practitioner to reduce undesirable behaviors. Since the goal was reduction of behaviors the number of baseline observations that were plotted below the celeration line, which are 4, are counted. If the opposite had been the case, and the practitioner's goal was to increase in some way a selected behavior of the client, then the number of observation points would be counted that fell above the celeration. Going back to Figure 4-4, a proportion of the total scores is then calculated. Since there are four plotted observation points that fall below the celeration line during the baseline period, the proportion of these four values in relation to the twelve total baseline values is obtained by dividing 4 by 12, yielding a quotient of .333.

7. Table 4-15 is used to determine whether the treatment has resulted in a statistically significant change, using the celeration line technique of analysis. The top horizontal row of numbers represent the total number of *treatment* observations. There were 16 treatment observations and, therefore, the number 16 on the top horizontal row of numbers is selected. Going down the vertical line of numbers under the label "Proportion from baseline observations" the value of .35 is also selected. Why .35 and not .33? Statistical tables are always read as conservatively as possible and since .333 is greater than .33 the next highest proportion is selected, which is .35. The intersect number in the body of the Table between 16 and .35 is 10. The value 10 is called a **critical value** and it establishes the minimum number of treatment observations that must fall below the estimation line if the change in undesirable behavior is to be considered statistically significant. This analysis, therefore, is found to be statistically significant because there are more than 10 observations, in fact there are 13, that fall below the estimation line. Table 4-15 will only provide information that enables the researcher to reject the hypothesis at a 5% level of significance. Essentially, this means there is a 5% possibility of rejecting the established null hypothesis and assuming that it is false when in fact it is really true.

Caveats to Keep in Mind When Using the Celeration Line Technique

Table 4-15 is a directional table because it is used when a treatment is expected to produce a change in the client's behavior. When data on any behavior that is being studied are expected to either decrease or increase as a result of a treatment, such data are considered to be directional in nature.

Directional data means that only one tail of a distribution is being used because the data are moving in that one direction, either increasing or decreasing. Directional data are evaluated by a *one-tailed test* because significance is determined from only one tail, either the negative or the positive portion, of the distribution. On the other hand a *two-tailed test* has no hypothesized directionality because it is not clear to the research-practitioner whether the data are moving one way or the other. The celeration line test is a means of predicting client change based upon the assumption that the data has directionality. Thus, Table 4-15 is a directional table and should not be used with the same probability

Table 4-15 Celeration Line Table[a]

Number of Treatment Observations

Proportion from baseline observations[b]	4	6	8	10	12	14	16	18	20	24	28	32	36	40	44	48	52	56	60	64	68	72	76	80	84	88	92	96	100
.05	2	2	3	3	3	3	3	4	4	4	4	5	5	5	6	6	6	7	7	7	8	8	8	8	9	9	9	10	10
.10	3	3	3	4	4	4	5	5	5	6	7	7	8	8	9	9	10	10	11	12	12	13	13	14	14	15	15	16	16
.125	3	3	4	4	5	5	5	6	6	7	8	8	9	10	10	11	12	12	13	14	14	15	15	16	17	17	18	19	19
.15	3	3	4	4	5	5	6	6	7	8	8	9	10	11	12	12	13	14	15	15	16	17	18	18	19	20	21	21	22
.17	3	4	4	5	5	6	6	7	7	8	9	10	11	12	13	13	14	15	16	17	18	18	19	20	21	22	22	23	24
.20	3	4	5	5	6	6	7	8	8	9	10	11	12	13	14	15	16	17	18	19	20	21	22	23	24	25	26	27	28
.25	4	4	5	6	7	7	8	9	9	11	11	12	14	16	17	18	19	20	22	23	24	25	26	27	29	30	31	32	33
.30	4	5	6	6	7	8	9	10	10	12	13	14	16	18	19	21	22	24	25	26	28	29	30	32	33	35	36	37	39
.33	4	5	6	7	8	9	9	10	11	13	15	16	18	19	21	22	24	26	27	29	30	32	33	35	36	38	39	41	42
.35	4	5	6	7	8	9	10	11	12	13	15	17	18	20	22	23	25	27	28	30	31	33	35	36	38	39	41	42	44
.375	4	5	6	7	8	9	10	11	12	14	16	18	19	21	23	25	26	28	30	31	33	35	36	38	40	42	43	45	47
.40	4	5	6	8	9	10	11	12	13	15	16	18	20	22	24	26	28	29	31	33	35	37	38	40	42	44	46	47	49

p	4	6	7	8	9	10	11	13	14	16	18	20	22	24	26	28	30	32	34	36	38	40	42	44	46	48	50	52	54
.45	4	6	7	8	9	10	11	13	14	16	18	20	22	24	26	28	30	32	34	36	38	40	42	44	46	48	50	52	54
.50	–	6	7	9	10	11	12	13	15	17	19	22	24	26	28	31	33	35	37	40	42	44	46	48	51	53	55	57	59
.55	–	6	8	9	10	12	13	14	16	18	21	23	26	28	31	33	35	38	40	43	45	48	50	52	55	57	59	62	64
.60	–	6	8	9	11	12	14	15	17	19	22	25	27	30	33	35	38	41	43	46	48	51	54	56	59	61	64	66	69
.625	–	–	8	10	11	13	14	16	17	20	23	25	28	31	34	36	39	42	45	47	50	53	55	58	61	63	66	69	71
.65	–	–	8	10	11	13	14	16	17	20	23	26	29	32	35	38	40	43	46	49	52	54	57	60	63	65	68	71	74
.667	–	–	8	10	12	13	15	16	18	21	24	27	30	32	35	38	41	44	47	50	53	55	58	61	64	67	70	72	75
.70	–	–	-	10	12	13	15	17	18	21	24	28	31	34	37	40	43	46	49	52	55	58	61	64	67	70	73	75	78
.75	–	–	–	–	12	14	16	17	19	22	26	29	32	35	39	42	45	48	51	55	58	61	64	67	70	74	77	80	83
.80	–	–	–	–	–	14	16	18	20	23	27	30	34	37	40	44	47	51	54	57	60	64	67	71	73	77	81	84	87
.833	–	–	–	–	–	–	–	18	20	24	27	31	34	38	42	45	49	52	56	59	63	66	69	73	76	80	83	87	90
.85	–	–	–	–	–	–	–	–	20	24	28	31	34	38	42	46	49	53	56	60	63	67	70	74	78	81	85	88	92
.875	–	–	–	–	–	–	–	–	–	24	28	32	36	39	43	47	50	54	57	61	65	68	72	76	79	83	86	90	94
.90	–	–	–	–	–	–	–	–	–	–	–	32	36	40	44	47	51	54	58	62	66	69	73	77	80	84	88	91	95
.95	–	–	–	–	–	–	–	–	–	–	–	–	–	–	–	–	52	56	60	64	68	72	76	79	83	87	91	95	99

[a] Alpha equals .05 on a one-tailed test

[b] If the proportion of baseline observations either above or below the celeration line does not appear in this table, use the next higher proportion. Also if the number of treatment observations is not shown use the next higher observation.

levels if a two-tailed, nondirectional hypothesis, is being tested. When the behavior under treatment has moved in a direction that is opposite from that which is hypothesized, then Table 4-15 can also be used to assess whether the values that are falling in the wrong direction are statistically significant. If the treatment is producing detrimental results, exactly opposite to what is desired, the data are considered to be non-directional and the probabilities on Table 4-15 must be doubled representing a 10% level of rejection.

Advantages and Disadvantages of the Celeration Line Technique

The celeration line is limited if the behavior that is being assessed during baseline reaches close to either a maximum or minimum that cannot be improved upon. A client cannot be expected to make improvements beyond a reasonable level. If that level has been reached, for whatever the reason may be during the baseline observations, the celeration line analysis will be of little value. Of course, if that is the case then treatment for the behavior would also be of questionable value because there would not be much room for improvement.

As was mentioned previously the minimum number of baseline observations should be no less than 10 and there should be at least 5 and preferably more treatment observations. Sometimes reality in the work setting prevents a practitioner from being able to obtain the minimum number of required baseline observations. The client may need immediate help and cannot wait around for the baseline observations to be completed. It is also possible that the client may not wish to be observed without help in the form of the planned treatment. Other mitigating circumstances could also prevent a professional worker from being able to complete the minimum number of baseline observations to calculate a celeration line. Under such circumstances it might be advisable to employ another method of analysis which uses the standard deviation of the distribution as a basis for determining significance of difference. This method, known as the *Shewart Chart Procedure*, will be discussed next.

THE SHEWART CHART PROCEDURE

This procedure by Shewart (1931) was an early development for use in industrial quality control. The original quality control procedure was later applied to the evaluation of educational programs (Gottman & Clasen, 1972). Shewart's procedure, also known as Shewart's Two Standard Deviation Band, is relatively uncomplicated and is based on the idea that observations taken over time will be statistically independent. There are certain assumptions associated with Shewart's Chart procedure. They are:

1. The assumption of random variation around some constant value, such as the mean. Variation that moves too far from the mean indicates that a significant change has occurred. While Shewart's procedure assumes there is randomness about a fixed value for a distribution of observations, this does not mean that the procedure is tolerant of serially related data. In fact, the Shewart method should *not* be used if data are autocorrelated.

2. This procedure is only appropriate for baseline data that have a relatively stable pattern. A stable pattern is one where neither wide fluctuatations nor persisting cycles are present.

3. Shewart's Chart methodology is weakened if the baseline data show a *trend* in behavior. A trend means that the data exhibits directionality. Data that are directional might be exemplified as either a continuous increase or decrease in the behavior being observed. Because of this limitation the Shewart procedure should not be used unless there are at least 15, and preferably 20 observations, indicating that a trend is *not* present.

If the above assumptions can be met the Shewart Chart procedure considers that a significant change has occurred when at least two successive observations fall beyond plus or minus two standard deviations from the mean of the distribution.

While the procedure is called the Two Standard Deviation Band, Shewart's approach can be used without standard deviation bands if the degree of observed shift exceeds an acceptable predetermined error limit. An example, using industrial quality control where error has been predetermined, is drawn from a coffee packaging company that must depend upon accurate net weight for each 12-ounce package that comes off the assembly line. To determine if the weight is accurate a sample of five packages are selected each day for a five-day period. If the company predetermines that it does not want the net weight of each package to vary by more than 1/8 of an ounce this weight would represent the predetermined tolerance limit. To carry out the quality control, each day a series of sample coffee packages would be selected based upon randomized hours. Each sample package would be weighed by an accurately calibrated independent scale and the results of the weighing would then be plotted. Figure 4-5 shows the weights of each sample package selected during random hours of each day of the week.

Note from the data in Figure 4-5 that beginning on Thursday the net weight of packages began to exceed the predetermined level of tolerance acceptable to the company. By Friday it was obvious that adjustments were needed in the procedure for filling the packages to assure that they were within acceptable weights.

Although the above example serves to demonstrate how the Shewart procedure can be used when there is a known and accepted predetermined level of error, Shewart's methodology can also be used when there may be uncertainty about the degree of error that can or should be accepted. What, for example, would be the predetermined tolerance level for a mentally retarded individual with aggressive behavior problems? It is possible to say that the ultimate long-term goal would be total, or near total, elimination of aggressive behavior. Shewart's approach, however, allows the practitioner-researcher to determine whether significant change is occurring before a final treatment goal has been reached. Significant change is considered to be present when two successive observations fall outside plus or minus two standard deviations of the distribution of treatment observations. If, during the treatment phase, two successive observations are found outside the two standard deviation band there is a 95% level of probability that the observed change is, in fact, "real" and cannot be attributed just to random variation in the data.

To continue with an example, the study of a mentally retarded person

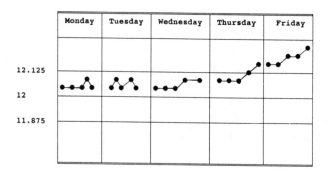

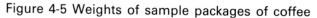

Figure 4-5 Weights of sample packages of coffee

indicated that he engaged in aggressive acts on an average of 7.733 times during daily, six hour observation periods, over a time span of 15 days. Two forms of aggressive acts were common and were the only ones included in the baseline observations. They were: (1) kicking, pushing or attacking property, e.g., knocking over chairs or tables and (2) pulling another person's hair. Table 4-16 shows the number of aggressive acts that were counted for each day of the baseline.

Procedural Steps to Calculate The Shewart Chart Procedure

The Shewart Chart procedure will be calculated using the following steps from the data in Table 4-16.

1. First the baseline data are graphed making sure that all of the previously mentioned assumptions have been observed. Figure 4-6 shows a graphing of the data found in Table 4-16.

Table 4-16 Aggressive Acts by Mentally Retarded Individual during Six-hour Observations for 15 Days

Day	1	2	3	4	5	6	7	8	9	10	11	12	13	14	15
Aggressive Acts	6	8	7	8	10	7	6	5	7	10	12	8	6	7	9

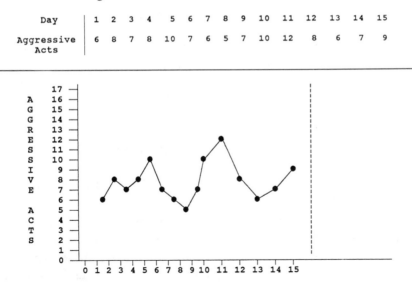

r_k = .31 – The data in this graph are not autocorrelated.

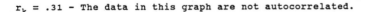

Figure 4-6 Baseline observations of aggressive acts of mentally retarded individual.

2. Next calculate the mean and then the standard deviation of the baseline data. The mean is calculated by summing all of the scores.

$$6 + 8 + 7 + 8 + 10 + 7 + 6 + 5 + 7 + 10 + 12 + 8$$
$$+ 6 + 7 + 9 = 116$$

Then dividing the sum of the scores by the number of observations in the distribution, in this case 15.

$$\frac{7.733}{15\sqrt{116.000}}$$

The mean $(\overline{X})$ for this distribution of observations is 7.733. The next step is to calculate the standard deviation as shown in Table 4-17. This is accomplished by subtracting the mean from every score in the distribution to obtain a deviation value, squaring the deviation value, summing the squared deviation values, dividing the sum of the squared deviations by $n - 1$ and then taking the square root of the quotient of that division. The calculations below follow the formula:

$$S = \sqrt{\frac{(X - \overline{X})^2}{n - 1}}$$

Where: S is the standard deviation

X is each score in the distribution

$\overline{X}$ is the mean of the distribution

n is the number in the distribution

The sum of the $(X - \overline{X})^2 = 50.51$. Dividing 50.51 by $(n - 1)$ which is $15 - 1$ or 14, yields a quotient of 3.61 and taking the square root of 3.61 gives 1.89 which is the standard deviation of the distribution.

3. Having calculated the standard deviation the next step is to draw a graph which shows the mean and also depicts two standard deviations above and two standard deviations below the mean. The two band deviation is calculated by multiplying the standard deviation, in this case 1.89, times 2 which yields a product of 3.78. Then 3.78 is both added to the mean of 7.733, to obtain the value for plus two standard deviations and subtracted from the mean of 7.733,

Table 4-17 Calculation of the Standard Deviation

Baseline Day	Number Aggressive Behaviors (X)	Number Minus The Mean $X - \bar{X}$	Number Minus The Mean Squared $(X - \bar{X})^2$
1	6	6 - 7.733 = -1.733	$(-1.733)^2 = 3.00$
2	8	8 - 7.733 = .267	$(.267)^2 = .07$
3	7	7 - 7.733 = -.733	$(-.773)^2 = .598$
4	8	8 - 7.733 = .267	$(.267)^2 = .07$
5	10	10 - 7.733 = 2.267	$(2.267)^2 = 5.15$
6	7	7 - 7.733 = -.733	$(-.773)^2 = .07$
7	6	6 - 7.733 = -1.733	$(-1.733)^2 = 3.00$
8	5	5 - 7.733 = -2.733	$(-2.733)^2 = 5.15$
9	7	7 - 7.733 = -.733	$(-.733)^2 = .07$
10	10	10 - 7.733 = 2.267	$(2.267)^2 = 5.15$
11	12	12 - 7.733 = 4.267	$(4.267)^2 = 18.21$
12	8	8 - 7.733 = .267	$(.267)^2 = .07$
13	6	6 - 7.733 = -1.733	$(-1.733)^2 = 3.00$
14	7	7 - 7.733 = -.733	$(-.733)^2 = .07$
15	9	9 - 7.733 = 1.267	$(1.267)^2 = 1.61$
			50.51

to obtain the value of minus two standard deviations. Figure 4-7 shows the two standard deviation band for the data.

4. After the mean of the baseline data and the two standard deviation bands have been drawn then the researcher continues graphing the data during the ''B'' phase while treatment is being given as shown in Figure 4-8.

5. As the data are being graphed the next step is to see if at least two successive observations drift either above or below the standard deviation band. In the Figure 4-8 note that one treatment observation has fallen below the -2 standard deviation band at day number 22, but day number 23 has an observation which is still within the standard deviation band. Therefore, no significance of difference has, as yet, been found. However, on days 24 and 25 the observations of behavior have declined to the point that there are two successive observed points that fall below the standard deviation band.

6. If at least two successive observations are found, during the treatment phase, to fall either above or below the standard deviation lines it can be said that a statistically significant shift (change) has taken place, which could occur by chance alone only 5 times in 100 and is accurate 95 times out of 100. Thus in the above example the treatment has produced a shift which is statistically significant at the 5% level of significance.

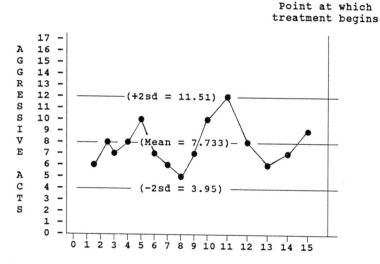

Figure 4-7 Baseline observations of aggressive acts of mentally retarded individual.

Advantages and Disadvantages of the Shewart Chart Procedure

The calculations for the Shewart procedure are simple and straightforward. While it is important to know whether statistically significant change of behavior has occurred the primary value of this procedure is to depict change in behavior rather than to prove statistical significance. Also, the Shewart procedure can be easily used for virtually all types of single subject designs that have distinct phases such as the A-B portion of the A-B-A-B design.

This procedure is, however, sensitive to autocorrelation problems so that before it is used the data should be tested to be sure that serial dependency is not present.

Having reviewed the Shewart Chart procedures, the next form of analysis to be covered is called the C statistic. The C statistic is a useful methodology for determining whether significant changes have occurred in level and direction between baseline and treatment observations.

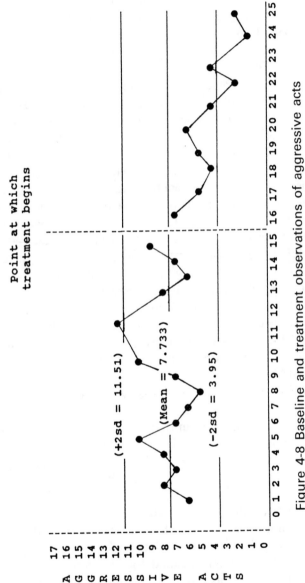

Figure 4-8 Baseline and treatment observations of aggressive acts of mentally retarded individual.

THE C STATISTIC

Autoregression is a process that has been developed for analysis of time series data. Gottman and Glass (1978) have described autoregression in considerable detail. The procedure is quite complicated mathematically. A widely used form of autoregression, presented by Box and Tiao (1965, 1975) and by Box and Jenkins (1970), is called ARIMA (Auto-Regressive Integrated Moving Averages). The ARIMA title denotes that this method of analysis integrates both moving averages processes with autoregression. The ARIMA form of time series analysis requires the building of empirical, mathematically developed, models that are based upon the available data. The model developed for a particular set of observations is used to extract serial dependency from that data, thereby adjusting the data to avoid autocorrelational problems. The construction of the model requires a relatively large number of observations. Glass, Wilson and Gottman, (1974) recommended a minimum of 50 observations. Box and Jenkins (1970) preferred 100 and Gottman, McFall and Barnett (1969) said that in fields outside of the behavioral sciences, such as engineering and economics, statisticians require about 200 observations before they feel comfortable. On the other hand, Jones, Vaught and Reid (1975) have written that, as a general rule, at least 10 data points should be available for each phase before the ARIMA is used. Obviously, there is a lack of agreement about the satisfactory minimum number of observations necessary to use the ARIMA approach.

The method is not without its problems for most practitioners. To begin with, so many observations as suggested by several authors, although possible in selected circumstances, would not be reasonable for single subject evaluation in the majority of clinical treatment programs. Another disadvantage is that the more the model mathematically reduces the number of data points the greater the chance will be of making a Type II error.

There is a statistic that can be used as a partial replacement for the ARIMA modeling approach, which is called the C statistic. The C statistic can be very helpful for the clinician in a human service setting because it provides a simple method for evaluating the effect of an intervention when as few as 8 observation points have been made. The major difference between the C statistic and the auto-regressive integrated moving averages method is that the ARIMA can assess abrupt changes in both **level** and **direction**. Level refers to a change in the frequency of the behavior between the baseline and the treatment. Direction estimates whether an immediate change at the exact point of intervention has occurred in the projected course of a targeted behavior. The C statistic's capacity is limited to evaluating abrupt changes in level that are accompanied by only gradual changes in direction. Figure 3-11 in Chapter 3 describes these concepts in more detail.

The Use of the C Statistic

One of the uses of the C statistic is to aid in determining whether or not a baseline contains a steady directional pathway. Additionally, the C statistic evaluates the difference between the baseline and treatment phases by comparing the direction of the slope found during the treatment phase with the direction of the slope found during the baseline period. If the difference between the two slopes is greater than what might be expected by chance alone then C will show that a statistically significant difference exists.

An example will help to further explain the C statistic and how it is calculated. A 15-year old mentally retarded girl was observed for two hours per day in her school classroom because she would not socially relate to other children. She refused to interact with her peers, especially during periods of free time. A study was conducted based upon two free time observation periods; one hour in the morning and one hour in the afternoon. She was observed for a five day period from Monday through Friday providing a baseline of ten observations. These data, which are displayed in Figure 4-9, represent the number of times the girl interacted with classmates. The treatment consisted of praise by the teacher each time the girl would interact socially with another child. The frequency of social contacts, in minutes, for both baseline and treatment phases was recorded by a trained observer.

The researcher's first question is whether the baseline data has consistent directionality, i.e., does the behavior show any systematic departure from random variation. For comparing the baseline with the treatment phase it is preferable that the baseline data should be random and should not show constancy of direction.

Procedural Steps for Calculating the C Statistic

The data from Figure 4-9 are shown under Column 1 in Table 4-18. The following are the steps for the calculation of the C statistic. It is

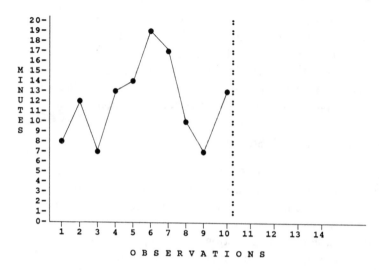

Figure 4-9 Baseline data showing frequency, in minutes, of social contacts with peers, during two single-hour free time periods per day, for a 15-year old mentally retarded girl.

suggested that the reader follow the information provided in Table 4-18 as the procedural steps are being described.

1. Obtain a baseline of observations and list these in tabular form as shown under Column 1 in Table 4-18.

2. Sum the observations in Column 1. For this problem the sum of the observations is 120.

3. Calculate the mean for the observations. The sum of the observations is 120 divided by n, which is 10, yields a mean of 12.

4. Subtract the first observed value from the second observed value, the second from the third, continuing the process until no numbers are left. List the remainders of each of the subtractions as shown in Column 2 of Table 4-18.

5. Square each of the difference values in Column 2 and establish the squares in Column 3. Sum the squared differences in Column 3. The sum of the squared differences for this example is 201. The squared Differences are symbolized as D^2, therefore $D^2 = 201$.

6. Subtract the mean of all observed values from each observed value. For this example the mean is 12 and 12 is subtracted from each value listed in Column 1. This step is symbolized as $(X - \overline{X})$ as

Table 4-18 Minutes of Social Interaction with Peers by a 15-year Old Mentally Retarded Girl

(1) Frequency (X)	(2) Difference between 1st & 2nd score, 2nd & 3rd score, etc.	(3) Difference squared	(4) $(X - \bar{X})$	(5) $(X - \bar{X})^2$
8	4	16	−4	16
12	−5	25	0	0
7	6	36	−5	25
13	1	1	1	1
14	5	25	2	4
19	−2	4	7	49
17	−7	49	5	25
10	−3	9	−2	4
7	6	36	−5	25
13		$D^2 = 201$	1	1
$\Sigma X = 120$				$\Sigma(X - \bar{X})^2 = 150$

$$\bar{X} = \frac{12}{10\overline{)120}}$$

Two single-hour observations per day using an A-B designed study

shown in Column 4 where X is any one observed value and $\bar{X}$ is the mean for all the observations.

7. Square all the values found in the column 4 $(X - \bar{X})$ and place the squared values into Column 5. Sum the squared deviations in Column 5. The value of the sum of squared deviations from the mean, symbolized as $(X - \bar{X})^2$ for this example, is 150. Multiply the sum of the squared deviations by 2 and for this example it is $2(150) = 300$.

8. Calculate the C statistic by the following formula.

$$C = 1 - \frac{D^2}{2(X - \bar{X})^2}$$

For this example it would be:

$$C = 1 - \frac{201}{300} = 1 - .67 = .33$$

In general a positive C value indicates a positive correlation between successive observations and, conversely, a negative C value shows an inverse relationship.

9. Calculate the Standard Error of Mean for the C statistic by using the following formula:

$$S_{\bar{x}} = \sqrt{\frac{n - 2}{(n - 1)(n + 1)}}$$

Using this formula for the example that is being calculated the standard error of the mean for the C statistic would be:

$$S_{\bar{x}} = \sqrt{\frac{10 - 2}{(10 - 1)(10 + 1)}} = \sqrt{\frac{8}{(9)(11)}} = .284$$

10. Calculate the Z value, which is based upon the ratio of the value of C to its standard error of the mean, using the following formula:

$$Z = \frac{C}{S_{\bar{x}}}$$

Using the example the Z value would be:

$$Z = \frac{.133}{.284} = 1.16$$

12. Having calculated the Z value, a determination can be made by referring to Table 4-19 as to whether there is a statistically significant constancy of direction through the baseline period or whether the data are randomly distributed. Table 4-19 provides critical values for the absolute value of C at the .01 and .05 alpha levels. The null hypothesis (H_0) is that the distribution of the baseline is random. To be able to reject the null hypothesis and state that the distribution has a constancy of direction or a trend, the calculated Z value of the C statistic must be larger than the critical value found in Table 4-19. The sample size is read on the left of the table and the intersect value at the .01 or .05 alpha levels represents the critical value for the specified level of significance. If the calculated Z value for C is larger than the critical value found in Table 4-19 the null hypothesis can be rejected. If the calculated Z value is smaller than the critical value the null hypothesis *cannot*

Table 4-19 Critical Values when Alpha Equals .01 and .05 for the Absolute Value of C Based on Selected Sample Sizes

Sample size, n	.01	.05
8	2.1664	1.6486
9	2.1826	1.6492
10	2.1958	1.6494
11	2.2068	1.6495
12	2.2161	1.6495
13	2.2241	1.6495
14	2.2310	1.6494
15	2.2369	1.6493
16	2.2423	1.6492
17	2.2470	1.6492
18	2.2513	1.6491
19	2.2550	1.6489
20	2.2585	1.6488
21	2.2616	1.6488
22	2.2647	1.6486
23	2.2676	1.6485
24	2.2700	1.6484
25	2.2717	1.6484
Infinity	2.3262	1.6447

Adapted from Table 1, L. C. Young, "On Randomness in Ordered Sequences," *Annals of Mathematical Statistics*, 1941, 12, 293–300.
*To reject the null hypothesis, the calculated Z value must be larger than the critical value found in this Table.

be rejected. Since the sample size for the example that has been worked is 10, the critical values are either 2.1958 for the .01 level or 1.6492 for the .05 level. The calculated Z value for the C statistic was 1.16, which does not exceed either of the critical values listed. Since the null hypothesis cannot be rejected, the assumption is made that there is no constancy of direction in the data. Therefore, the data are random in nature.

Having determined that the baseline does not have a constant direction the next concern is to compare the baseline with observations taken during treatment. There were five days of baseline or 10 observations and 10 days of treatment or 20 observations, totaling 30 observations. The treatment observations are shown appended to the baseline observations in Figure 4-10. The entire set of data for both the baseline and treatment phases is calculated using the same steps that were used to calculate constancy of direction during the baseline period. The mean

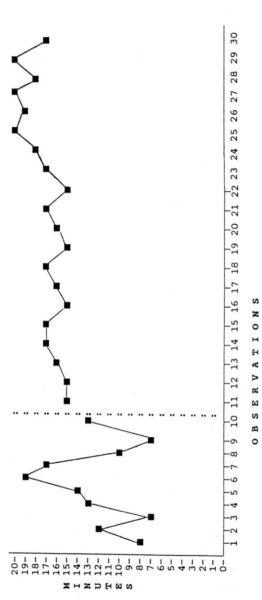

Figure 4-10 Baseline data showing frequency, in minutes, of social
contacts with peers, during two single hour free time periods per
day, for a 15-year old mentally retarded girl.

is calculated from all 30 observations, as are the difference values (D) and the deviation values $(X - \overline{X})$.

Table 4-20 shows the calculations of the mean, the sum of the squared differences and the sum of the deviations values of each value from the mean, for both the baseline (A) and treatment phases (B).

Thus for the baseline of 10 observations along with the appended treatment observations, the following calculations will indicate whether a statistically significant difference exists between the two phases.

$$D^2 = 407$$

$$2(X - \overline{X})^2 = 2(436) = 872$$

$$C = 1 - \frac{D^2}{2(X - \overline{X})^2} = 1 - \frac{407}{872} = 1 - .4667 = .5333$$

$$S_{\overline{X}} = \sqrt{\frac{n - 2}{(n - 1)(n + 1)}}$$

$$= \sqrt{\frac{30 - 2}{(30 - 1)(30 + 1)}}$$

$$= \sqrt{\frac{28}{(29)(31)}}$$

$$= \sqrt{\frac{28}{899}}$$

$$= \sqrt{.031} = .177$$

$$Z = \frac{.5333}{.177} = 3.01$$

The null hypothesis (H_0) for this research is "the treatment had no demonstrable effect upon the socialization behavior of the child." If the null hypothesis can be rejected then the alternate hypothesis (H_1) is *not* rejected, which states "there is a statistically significant difference in the child's behavior between baseline and treatment observations."

Comparing the calculated Z value with the appropriate critical value found in Table 4-19, which is Infinity because the sample size is over 25, the critical value is found to be 2.3262 at alpha equals .01. Since

Table 4-20 Minutes of Social Interaction with Peers for a 15-year Old Mentally Retarded Girl

(1) Frequency	(2) Difference between 1st & 2nd score, 2nd & 3rd score, etc.	(3) Difference squared	(4) $(X - \bar{X})$	(5) $(X - \bar{X})^2$
8			-7	49
12	4	16	-3	9
7	-5	25	-8	64
13	6	36	-2	4
14	1	1	-1	1
19	5	25	4	16
17	-2	4	2	4
10	-7	49	-5	25
7	-3	9	-8	64
13	6	36	-2	4
15	2	4	0	0
15	0	0	0	0
16	1	1	1	1
17	1	1	2	4
17	0	0	2	4
15	-2	4	0	0
16	1	1	1	1
17	1	1	2	4
15	-2	4	0	0
16	1	1	1	1
17	1	1	2	4
15	-2	4	0	0
17	2	4	2	4
18	1	1	3	9
20	2	4	5	25
19	-1	1	4	16
18	-1	1	3	9
20	2	4	5	25
20	0	0	5	25
17	-13	169	-8	64
450		407		436

$$\frac{15 = \bar{X}}{30)450}$$

Two single-hour free time periods using an A-B designed study the calculated Z value is larger than the critical value of Z, the null hypothesis is rejected and the finding is that there has, in fact, been a statistically significant change in the constancy of the directional pathway of the child's behavior. The statistical finding is essentially confirmed by visually inspecting the data in Figure 4-10. Note that the baseline (A phase) shows erratic behavior that follows no particular direction and was confirmed by the C statistic as being random in nature. Inspecting the treatment (B) phase on Figure 4-10 shows how the socialization behavior has improved and indicates that there is a continuous ascending direction of social contacts displayed during the treatment observations.

This statistic can also be used to evaluate extensions of the A-B design. While the number of calculations increases, the same procedure is followed as the data from each phase are added to the previous phase(s).

Advantages and Disadvantages of the C Statistic

The C statistic is a relatively easy, yet fairly accurate method for determining the presence of changes resulting from a treatment intervention when the data may be serially dependent. The use of C does not require determination of autocorrelation in the data.

The C statistic, can be used as a substitute for the ARIMA, but it should be recognized that it cannot evaluate abrupt changes in level separately from changes in direction. It can, however, assess abrupt changes in level of data when accompanied with gradual changes in the direction of the data.

C can be used with as few as eight observations, which makes it a useful statistic for clinicians in human service settings. It does not require the use of computer modeling and can be calculated using a hand calculator.

Blumberg (1984) has questioned some of the results obtained by the C statistic as being of function of the number of data points in the series and not the slope. It is true that the power of this statistic is directly proportional to the number of data points in the series so that in this sense C is a function of the sample size. The more the data points the more powerful the analysis. Thus, statistical significance is more likely to occur when baseline as well as treatment data points are used as opposed to using either baseline or treatment points alone.

The C statistic is a reasonably reliable measure for establishing the probability that a time series is random. Rejecting the null hypothesis indicates that a trend is present in the data. When the treatment data are joined to the baseline the C statistic provides adequately accurate information about changes in slope that occur at the point of treatment.

TRANSFORMING AUTOCORRELATED DATA

Transforming serially related data is a method used to lessen or diminish the degree of autocorrelation in the data by mathematical manipulation. Serial dependency causes as much of a problem in graphing information, resulting in spurious interpretation, as it does with statistical analysis. How does the research-practitioner handle graphing information or statistical analysis if the calculation of Bartlett's test provides data that are serially related? From among several approaches there are two different ways that will be discussed of "smoothing" the original data to remove the relationship between succeeding values. One way is called the *first differences transformation* and the other is the *moving average transformation* (Gottman and Leiblum, 1974). Both of these methods help the researcher to reduce the degree of oscillation of data, thus making interpretation more reliable.

First Differences Transformation

The first difference transformation is most appropriate when the autocorrelated data appear to follow a relatively straight ascending or descending line. A straight line that moves diagonally either upward or downward represents directional data. Data that are linear in nature and do not vary around a constant value, such as the mean, do not meet one of the assumptions necessary for independence. Independence requires that the data display essentially uniform variability over all observations. If there is a general linear direction or path taken by the data, and they are autocorrelated, than the use a *first difference transformation* should be considered.

Procedural Steps for Calculating a First Differences Transformation

A first differences transformation will be calculated for Figure 4-11 which is based upon hypothetical data.

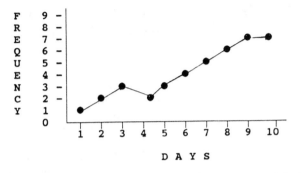

Figure 4-11 Hypothetical data showing frequency of behavior by days.

1. List the data that have been gathered. The data from Figure 4-11 are displayed as:

$$1, 2, 3, 2, 3, 4, 5, 6, 7, 7$$

2. Calculate to determine if the original observations are independent. Using the r_k procedure to calculate autocorrelation it is found that the original data are, in fact, autocorrelated. Bartlett's ratio is 1.09 which is larger than the absolute value of 1 ($|1|$).

3. The data ascend directionally, are autocorrelated, and would not be appropriately used for graphing analysis. It appears reasonable, therefore, to transform the data using a "first differences transformation." To accomplish the transformation, list the data in tabular form as shown in Table 4-21.

4. Subtract the first value from the second, the second from the third, until no further subtraction is possible. The procedure is shown in column 3 of Table 4-21.

5. Calculate Bartlett's ratio (B_r) to determine whether the transformed data, as shown in Column 3, are still autocorrelated. Table 4-21 shows that r_k has been calculated to be -0.1944. Bartlett's ratio is calculated by dividing r_k by $2/\sqrt{n}$. Thus, $-0.1944/\sqrt{9} = -0.1944/3 = -0.2917$. Since -0.2917 is less than the absolute value of 1 ($|1|$), the data, using the *first difference transformation* are no longer autocorrelated.

6. If the data are still dependent, consider using a second transformation.

Table 4-21 Calculation of First Differences for Original Autocorrelated Data

1 Order	2 Score	3 1st score minus second, 2nd minus third, etc.	4 Calculate Bartlett's r
1st	1	2 − 1 = 1	Follow the
2nd	2	3 − 2 = 1	same steps
3rd	3	2 − 3 = −1	as shown on
4th	2	3 − 2 = 1	page 58.
5th	3	4 − 3 = 1	
6th	4	5 − 4 = 1	
7th	5	6 − 5 = 1	$r_k = -0.1944$
8th	6	7 − 6 = 1	
9th	7	7 − 7 = 0	
10th	7		

Now compare Figure 4-12, the transformed data, with the data from Figure 4-11 where the data were not transformed. Note that the transformed data are now considerably more uniform and are much more unvarying in appearance. The data are considered to be "smoothed."

Although the initial calculation of "first differences" yielded transformed data that are not autocorrelated there are times when the data remain serially dependent. Under such circumstances a second transformation can be used in which the first score is subtracted from the

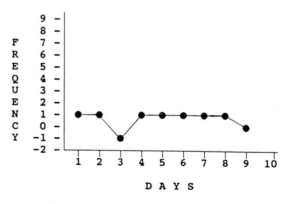

Figure 4-12 Smoothing of data

third score, the second from the fourth, the third from the fifth, etc. Generally, there is a diminishing value in continuing to calculate beyond the second transformation. If the second transformation continues to yield autocorrelated data, then it might be advisable to consider using another method such as the *moving averages transformation.*

Moving Averages Transformation

Another method that the research practitioner may find useful for reducing the oscillation of the data is called the *moving average transformation.* This method is different from the "first differences transformation" in that it averages successive observations. For example, two successive days of measurements can be averaged, or three days, or a whole week of observations. The number of successive combinations of observations that are averaged depend in great part on common sense and the nature of the data. This method is especially useful for reducing erratic data.

The "moving average transformation" decreases the degree of irregularity in the data and makes the graph easier to interpret. This can be exemplified by looking at Figure 4-13. Note that Figure 4-13(a) has rather wide swings in the data. If, however, each successive pair of observations are averaged and then plotted, the distribution is "smoothed" as seen in Figure 4-13(b). Day 1 with a value of 2 added to the value in day 2 which is 6 yields an average of 4. Similarly day 3 with a value of 2 added to day 4 with a value of 6, again yields an average of 4. Each of the two successive values average to 4, thus producing a straight line from the previously variable data.

A more practical example may be in order. In Figure 4-14 a clinician working with a depressed client administered a Depression Scale over a 7 week baseline period after which the clinician began treatment. The baseline depression scores were plotted twice a week. The depressions scores were:

Week 1-21 and 23   Week 5-25 and 28
Week 2-22 and 24   Week 6-27 and 28
Week 3-24 and 25   Week 7-29 and 29
Week 4-26 and 27

The calculation of lag 1 autocorrelation for the original data indicated an *r* of .6450. Bartlett's ratio was 1.2067, a value greater than the absolute value of 1. Therefore, this data set during baseline observa-

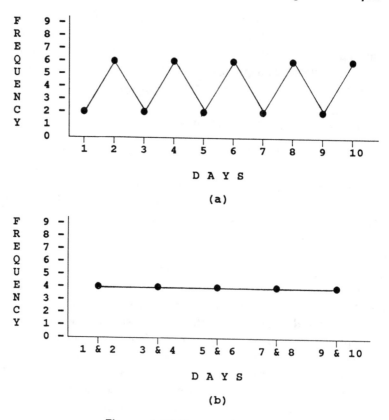

Figure 4-13 Data variability

tions, was autocorrelated. The original data has been plotted in Figure 4-14.

Since these data were autocorrelated, they cannot be reliably used either for graphing or for statistical analysis. As mentioned previously, there are other procedures in addition to the two being described that can be employed to transform the autocorrelated data to achieve independence. Transforming the data, however, has its negative effects because some of the original information is lost. Also, the smaller the number of observations resulting from the transformation of the original data, the greater the likelihood that Bartlett's test will show independence in the data. As a general rule of thumb it is best that at least six, and preferably more, transformed values should be available for evaluation to avoid finding questionable evidence of independence in the data.

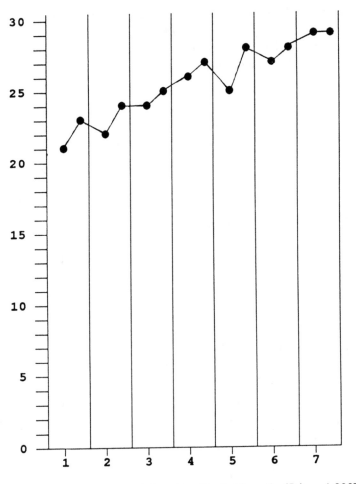

Autocorrelation r = .6450 (lag 1) – Bartlett's ratio (B$_r$) = 1.2067

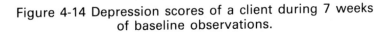

Figure 4-14 Depression scores of a client during 7 weeks of baseline observations.

The two successively plotted points each representing one week of observations are:

Week 1-(21 + 23)/2 = 22   Week 5-(25 + 28)/2 = 26.5
Week 2-(22 + 24)/2 = 23   Week 6-(27 + 28)/2 = 27.5
Week 3-(24 + 25)/2 = 24.5   Week 7-(29 + 29)/2 = 29
Week 4-(26 + 27)/2 = 26.5

Figure 4-15 shows the Moving Average Transformation of the 7 weeks of clinical depression scores. In Figure 4-15 note that the number of plotted points have been reduced from the original 14 shown in Figure 4-14 to 7, because successively paired observations were averaged.

Practitioners should be alert to one disadvantage of the moving av-

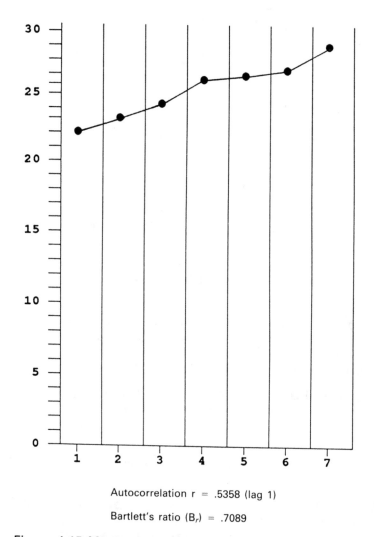

Autocorrelation r = .5358 (lag 1)

Bartlett's ratio (B_r) = .7089

Figure 4-15 Moving average transformation of data from Figure 4-14 plotted on a new graph.

erages transformation. When data are combined or averaged it is true that stability will tend to emerge. Some of the detail concerning the observations is, however, always lost. Aggregating daily data into a weekly unit will disguise the daily variability just as combining hourly observations into daily units will camouflage the detailed information about the hours.

OTHER RANDOMIZATION PROCEDURES

Edgington (1987) has described a number of randomization procedures, most requiring computer analysis. This section is offered as a brief introduction for the reader who wishes to learn more about randomization tests.

All randomization tests are based upon permutations where a test statistic is calculated for each randomized permutation. A randomization test is a permutation test that is based upon *random assignment*. The procedure for randomization tests is to calculate a statistic for the treatment data, after which the treatment data are rearranged into permutations. The same statistic is then computed for each of the permutations. These permutations, including the treatment permutation, are used for determining whether the treatment effect was statistically significant.

While randomization tests require *random assignment* they do not depend upon *random sampling*. At one time it was also thought that random sampling was a necessary procedure to carry out a randomization test, but it is now recognized that these tests are valid for any type of sample whether randomly or nonrandomly selected.

An example will provide information about the method of calculation for one form of randomized test. This example is primarily to demonstrate the procedure because it has an arbitrarily small sample size. The usefulness of the test in this example is limited because there should be more than 10 ways that the data can be permuted. If there are too few available permutations the researcher is unable to reject the null hypothesis at an acceptable alpha level.

The null hypothesis for most randomization tests is that the subject's response will not be effected by the treatment. If the null hypothesis can be rejected then it can be said that the treatment did have an effect.

For this example, five cynophobic individuals were randomly assigned to two treatments as a method for reducing their phobic reaction to being in proximity with a dog. Time was measured in seconds while a small dog was kept exposed in the same room with each of these subjects. There were two treatment approaches. The first consisted of providing the subject with a preset time limit which was established cooperatively with the clinician. The subject, knew the number of seconds that would meet acceptable criteria, but was not provided with information as to the length of time that was transpiring during the experimental exposure. The second treatment consisted of providing continuous feedback in which each subject was told, during the period of exposure to the dog, how he or she was progressing in extending the toleration time.

The five individuals, alphabetically listed, were Ann (A), Burt (B), Carl (C), David (D) and Elaine (E). Each person was considered to have been randomly assigned to one or the other of the two treatments. Three individuals were randomly assigned to the first treatment and two to the second treatment. The data are provided in seconds for the length of time that each subject could look at the dog without requesting its removal. By means of a random selection procedure the data were collected for the one permutation—the ADE BC permutation. This permutation required that Ann, David and Elaine be given the first treatment and Burt and Carl the second treatment. Data obtained for the randomly selected permutation are provided in Figure 4-16. The use of the treatment data for all other permutations, including the treatment permutation ADE BC is shown in Figure 4-17.

The first step for calculating this randomization test is to take the data from Figure 4-16 and assign it to each of the permutations. The ADE BC permutation, during which treatment was provided, shows that Ann could tolerate the dog for 15 seconds, David 7 seconds, Elaine 11 seconds, Burt 20 seconds, and Carl 34 seconds. Using the data from this permutation, values are then assigned to each individual for all of the other permutations. For example, the first permutation shown in

Subject 1	Subject 2	Subject 3	Subject 4	Subject 5
Ann (A)	David (D)	Elaine (E)	Burt (B)	Carl (C)
15	7	11	20	34

Figure 4-16 Treatment permutation showing exposure times in seconds for five cynophobic subjects.

		Ann	Burt	Carl	David	Elaine	(ABC DE)
$\bar{X}=$	23.00	15	20	34	7	11	$\bar{X} = 9.00$
t=	|1.87|						
		Ann	Burt	David	Carl	Elaine	(ABD CE)
$\bar{X} =$	14.00	15	20	7	34	11	$\bar{X} = 22.50$
t =	|.86|						
		Ann	Burt	Elaine	Carl	David	(ABE CD)
$\bar{X} =$	15.33	15	20	11	34	7	$\bar{X} = 20.5$
t =	|-.49|						
		Ann	Carl	David	Burt	Elaine	(ACD BE)
$\bar{X} =$	18.67	15	34	7	20	11	$\bar{X} = 15.5$
t =	|.29|						
		Ann	Carl	Elaine	Burt	David	(ACE BD)
$\bar{X} =$	20.00	15	34	11	20	7	$\bar{X} = 13.5$
t =	|.63|						
		Ann	David	Elaine	Burt	Carl	(ADE BC)
$\bar{X} =$	11.00	15	7	11	20	34	$\bar{X} = 27.0$
t =	|-2.66|						
		Burt	Carl	David	Ann	Elaine	(BCD AE)
$\bar{X} =$	20.33	20	34	7	15	11	$\bar{X} = 13.0$
t =	|.72|						
		Burt	Carl	Elaine	Ann	David	(BCE AD)
$\bar{X} =$	21.67	20	4	11	15	7	$\bar{X} = 11.0$
t =	|1.17|						
		Burt	David	Elaine	Ann	Carl	(BDE AC)
$\bar{X} =$	12.67	20	7	11	15	34	$\bar{X} = 24.5$
t =	|1.17|						
		Carl	David	Elaine	Ann	Burt	(CDE AB)
$\bar{X} =$	17.33	34	7	11	15	20	$\bar{X} = 17.5$
t =	|.02|						

Figure 4-17 Permutations of data for five cynophobic subjects

Figure 4-17 is Ann, Burt, Carl, David and Elaine or ABC DE and values from the treatment permutation found in Figure 4-16 are assigned, for this example, to the letters representing each of the individuals. The second permutation is ABD CE and similarly values are assigned from the treatment permutation to the ABD CE permutation. This is done for all ten permutations in this example.

The question may arise as to how the value of 10 was obtained for the number of possible permutations. The formula is:

$$_5P_{3,2} = \frac{5!}{3!2!} = 10 \text{ possible permutations}$$

The above equation represents a permutation for five subjects who have been randomly assigned to two treatments in which three of the subjects were assigned to one treatment and two to the other.

The calculating procedure is to list the numerator as:

$5 \times 4 \times 3 \times 2 \times 1$ and the denominator as: $(3 \times 2 \times 1)(2 \times 1)$

$$\text{or } \frac{5 \times 4 \times 3 \times 2 \times 1}{(3 \times 2 \times 1)(2 \times 1)}$$

The denominator portion of the equation, which is $3 \times 2 \times 1$ is divided into the numerator portion of $3 \times 2 \times 1$. The procedure cancels these values out leaving:

$$\frac{5 \times 4 \times 3 \times 2 \times 1}{(3 \times 2 \times 1)(2 \times 1)} = \frac{5 \times 4}{2 \times 1} = \frac{20}{2} = 10 \text{ possible permutations}$$

Then the independent t test, whose method of calculation was explained from pages 61 to 66, was used. The t test is one of several types of statistics that can be used to determine whether the treatment permutation had a significant effect. For example, the Mann-Whitney U, a nonparametric statistic which was explained from pages 68 to 75, could also have been used instead of the parametric t test. It should be noted from Figure 4-17 that observed t values are considered to be absolute values without regard to their sign. Once the absolute observed values for the t statistic were calculated for each permutation, they were then ordered from high to low. This ordering of the t values creates a hypothetical distribution of t for the sample. The level of significance for a two tailed test is obtained by adding the number of absolute t values in the ordered distribution that are larger than the t value for the treatment permutation. That sum is then divided into the number of permutations to provide the significance level of the findings for the study. The procedural steps that follow provide a more in-depth explanation.

Procedural Steps

1. Select the number of subjects and the number of different types of treatments that will be administered. For this example there were five subjects and two different treatments.

2. Calculate and establish a list of the maximum number of permutations. This example had five subjects, three of whom were assigned to one treatment and two to the other, making for 10 possible permutations.

3. Make a list of all possible permutations and then randomly select one of the permutations which will dictate the arrangement of the subjects during treatment. For this example the treatment was carried out following the order of arrangement of the BCD AE permutation. This meant that the second, third and fourth subjects (Burt "B," Carl "C," David "D") were used for treatment one, and the first and fifth subjects (Ann "A," and Elaine "E") were given the second treatment.

6. After gathering the data for the treatment permutation, incorporate that data into the entire listing of permutations.

7. Calculate the observed values for an appropriately selected statistical test and list these values for each permutation. In the instance of this example, the independent t test was used, and the absolute values of the observed t for each permutation were calculated.

8. The observed values of the statistic are then ordered from high to low. For this example they are: $|-2.66|$, $|1.87|$, $|1.17|$, $|1.17|$, $|.86|$, $|.72|$, $|.63|$, $|-.49|$, $|.29|$, $|.02|$.

9. Looking at Figure 4-17 it can be seen that the treatment permutation ADE BC had the highest absolute observed t value of $|-2.66.|$. There are no other permutations as high as the treatment permutation. Therefore, for a two-tailed probability, one, representing the treatment permutation alone, is divided by ten representing the total number of permutations. The probability of being able to reject the null hypothesis that the treatment had no statistical effect upon the subjects is $\dfrac{1}{10} = .10$

As stated when first characterizing this statistic, if the number of permutations is as small as 10, an acceptable alpha level for rejection of the null hypothesis is not attainable. A 10% level of rejection is generally an unsuitable level of significance for rejection of the null hypothesis in the behavioral sciences. Yet the 10% level was the highest attainable level for this problem. If one of the other permutations would have had an absolute t value greater than the treatment permutation than both the treatment permutation and the one higher permutation would have meant that there were two values to be divided by 10 which would then have provided an even more unacceptable level of rejection at 20%. The more the number of permutations the greater the potential for being able to reject the null hypothesis at a .05 or higher alpha level. Generally it is preferable for the number of permutations to exceed 10, but computer analysis becomes necessary to determine the permutations. Programs are available in certain texts that enable the researcher to use the computer to generate the necessary number of permuations (Edgington, 1987).

Advantages and Disadvantages of Randomization Tests

Randomization tests do not require that the assumptions for traditional inferential statistical tests must be upheld. Randomization procedures are distribution free because they make no assumptions that require the population to be either normally distributed or the sample to be representative on the basis of random selection. Autocorrelation of data is not a problem when using randomization tests since the hypothesis of "no difference" should be found to be equally present for all permutations.

Randomization tests are disadvantageous because the researcher cannot generalize to a population of interest as is the case when using conventional statistics requiring random selection. Therefore, no inferences can be made about other "similar" types of subjects with randomization tests. If such inferences are made they cannot be justified on the basis of any reasonable level of probability but only by means of nonstatistical procedures. Generally, the form of behavior that is treated when randomization tests are used should be reversible. When behavior is irreversible randomization tests are not applicable. In addition, while serially related behavioral data for a single subject does not pose a problem with randomization tests, serially related treatments may create a problem. The problem could be caused by one treatment affecting a succeeding treatment resulting in a "carry-over" effect.

Another adverse characteristic of randomization tests are the computations required for numerous permutations. To reduce the problem of calculating permutations, Edgington (1987) has provided a number of Fortran IV computer programs throughout his book that can either be copied or translated into other computer languages.

REFERENCES

Barlow, D. H., D. Blanchard, S. C. Hayes, and L. Epstein. "Single Case Designs and Clinical Biofeedback Experimentation." *Biofeedback and Self-Regulation*, 1977, 2, pp. 211–236.

Barlow, D. H. and S. C. Hayes. "Alternating Treatment Design: One Strategy for Comparing the Effects of Two Treatments in a Single Subject." *Journal of Applied Behavior Analysis*, 1979, 12, 199–210.

Barlow, D. H., and M. Hersen. "Single Case Experimental Designs: Uses in Applied Clinical Research." *Archives of General Psychiatry*, 1973, 29, pp. 319–325.

Barlow, D. H., and M. Hersen. *Single Case Experimental Designs: Strategies for Studying Behavior Change*. New York: Pergamon Press, 1984.

Barnard, G. A. "Discussion of Professor Bartlett's Paper." *Journal of the Royal Statistical Society*, Series B, 1963, 25, p. 294.

Bergin, A. E. "Some Implications of Psychotherapy Research for Therapeutic Practice." *Journal of Abnormal Psychology*, 1966, 71, pp. 235–246.

Bergin, A. and H. Strupp. "New Directions in Psychotherapy Research." *Journal of Abnormal Psychology*, 1970, 76, pp. 13–26.

Bloom, M. and J. Fischer. *Evaluating Practice: Guidelines for the Accountable Professional*. Englewood Cliffs, NJ: Prentice-Hall, 1982.

Blumberg, C. J. Comments on "A Simplified Time-Series Analysis for Evaluating Treatment Interventions" *Journal of Applied Behavior Analysis*, 1984, 17, pp. 539–542.

Boring, E. G. *Sensation and Perception in the History of Experimental Psychology*. New York: Appleton-Century, 1942.

Box, G. E. P., and G. M. Jenkins. *Time Series Analysis: Forecasting and Control*. San Francisco: Holden-Day, 1970.

Box, G. E. P., and G. C. Tiao. "A Change in Level of Non-stationary Time Series." *Biometrika*, 1965, 52, pp. 181–199.

Box, G. E. P., and G. C. Tiao. "Intervention Analysis with Applications to Economic and Environmental Problems." *Journal of the American Statistical Association*, 1975, pp. 70–92.

Briar, S. "Research and Practice: Partners in Social Work Knowledge Development," in *Toward Human Dignity: Social Work In Practice*. Ed. J. W. Hanks. Washington, D.C.: National Association of Social Workers, 1978.

Bryan, W. L. and N. Harter. "Studies on the Telegraphic Language. The Acquisition of a Hierarchy of Habits. *Psychological Review*, 1899, 6, pp. 345–375.

Campbell, D. T. and J. C. Stanley. *Experimental and Quasi-Experimental Designs for Research*. Chicago: Rand McNally & Company, 1963.

Cannon, W. B. and A. L. Washburn. "An Explanation of Hunger." *American Journal of Physiology*, 1912, 29, pp. 441–454.

Cook, T. D. and T. D. Campbell. *Quasi-Experimentation: Design and Analysis Issues for Field Settings*. Chicago: Rand McNally & Company, 1979.

Crosbie, J. "The Inability of the Binomial Test to Control Type I Error with Single-Subject Data." *Behavioral Assessment*, 1987, 9, pp. 141–150.

DeProspero, A. and S. Cohen. "Inconsistent Visual Analysis of Intrasubject Data." *Journal of Applied Behavior Analysis*, 1979, 12, pp. 573–579.

Dukes, W. F. "N = 1." *Psychological Bulletin*, 1965, 64, pp. 74–79.

Ebbinghaus, H. "*Uber das Gedachtnis: Untersachungen Zur Experimentelen Psychologie*. Leipzig: Duncher and Humbolt, 1885.

Edgington, E. S. "Validity of Randomization Tests." *Journal of Educational Statistics*, 1980, 5, pp. 235–251.

Edgington, E. S. *Randomization Tests* (2nd. ed.). New York: Marcel Dekker, 1987.

Eysenck, J. "The Effects of Psychotherapy: An Evaluation." *Journal of Consulting Psychology*, 1952, 16, pp. 319–324.

Fisher, R. A. *The Design of Experiments* (6th ed.), New York: Hafner, 1951.

Furlong, M. J. and B. Wampold. "Visual Analysis of Single-Subject Studies by School Psychologists." *Psychology in the Schools*. 1981, 18, pp. 80–86.

Gingerich, W. J. "Procedure of Evaluating Clinical Practice." *Health and Social Work*, 1979, 4, pp. 105–130.

Glass, G. V., V. L. Wilson, and J. M. Gottman. *Design and Analysis of Time Series Experiments*. Boulder, Col.: Colorado Associated University Press, 1974.

Gottman, J. M. and R. M. Clasen. *Evaluation in Education: A Practitioner's Guide*. Itasca, Ill: Peacock Press, 1972.

Gottman, J. M. and G. V. Glass. "Analysis of Interrupted Time-series Experiments." In: *Single-subject Research: Strategies for Evaluating Change*. T. R. Kratochwill (Ed.) New York: Academic Press, 1978, pp. 197–235.

Gottman, J. M. and S. R. Leiblum. *How to do Psychotherapy and How to Evaluate It*. New York: Holt, Rinehart and Winston, 1974.

Gottman, J. M., R. M. McFall, and J. T. Barnett. "Design and Analysis of Research Using Time Series." *Psychological Bulletin*, 1969, pp. 299–306.

Harris, F. N., and W. R. Jensen. "Comparisons of Multiple-Baseline Across Persons Designs and AB Designs with Replication: Issues and Confusions." *Behavioral Assessment*, 1985, 4, pp. 121–127.

Hartmann, D. P., and R. V. Hall. "A Discussion of the Changing Criterion Design." *Journal of Applied Behavioral Analysis*, 1976, 9, pp. 527–532.

Hersen, M. "Single-Case Experimental Designs." In *International Handbook of Behavior Modification and Therapy*. Eds. A. S. Bellack, M. Hersen, and A. E. Kazdin. New York: Plenum, 1982, pp. 167–201.

Hersen, M. and D. H. Barlow. *Single Case Experimental Designs: Strategies for studying Behavior Change*, New York, Pergamon Press, 1976.

Hersen, M. and D. H. Barlow. *Single Case Experimental Designs: Strategies for Studying Behavior Change*. (2nd ed.) New York: Pergamon Press, 1984.

Hudson, W. W. "Elementary Techniques for Assessing Single Client/Single Worker Interactions." *Social Service Review*, June 1977, pp. 311–326.

Jayaratne, S. "Single Subject and Group Designs." *Social Work Research and Abstracts*, 14, 1978, pp. 30–40.

Johnson, J. and H. Pennypacker. *Strategies and Tactics of Human Behavior Research*. Hillsdale, N.J.: Erlbaum, 1980.

Jones, Mary C. "A Laboratory Study of Fear: The Case of Peter." *Journal of Genetic Psychology*, 1924, 31, pp. 308–315.

Jones, R. R., R. S. Vaught, and J. B. Reid. "Time Series Analysis as a Substitute for Single Subject Analysis of Variance Designs." In: G. R. Patterson, I. M. Marks, J. D. Matarazzo, R. A. Myers, G. E. Schwarts, and H. H. Strupp (Eds.) *Behavior Change.* 1975, Chicago, Aldine, pp. 164–169.

Jones, R. R., R. S. Vaught, and M. R. Weinrott. "Time Series Analysis in Operant Research." *Journal of Applied Behavior Analysis,* 1977, 10, pp. 151–167.

Jones, R. R., M. R. Weinrott, and R. S. Vaught. "Effects of Serial Dependency on Agreement Between Visual and Statistical Inference." *Journal of Applied Behavior Analysis,* 1978, 11, pp. 277–283.

Kaestner, N. F. and H. L. Ross. "Highway Safety Programs: How Do We Know They Work?" *North Carolina Symposium on Highway Safety,* 1974, pp. 1–67.

Kazdin, A. E. *Behavior Modification in Applied Settings.* Homewood, Ill.: Dorsey Press, 1975.

Kazdin, A. E. "Statistical Analyses for Single-Case Experimental Designs." In M. Hersen and D. H. Barlow (Eds.). *Single-Case Experimental Designs: Strategies for Studying Behavior Change.* New York: Pergamon Press, 1976.

Kazdin, A. E. and S. Geesey. "Simultaneous-Treatment Design Comparisons of the Effects of Earning Reinforcers for One's Peers Versus for Oneself." *Behavior Therapy,* 1977, 8, pp. 682–693.

Kazdin, A. E. and D. P. Hartmann. "The Simultaneous-Treatment Design." *Behavior Therapy,* 1978, 5, pp. 912–923.

Kellogg, W. N., and Luella Kellogg. *The Ape and the Child.* New York: McGraw-Hill, 1933.

Kelly, F. J., K. McNeil, and I. Newman. "Suggested Inferential Statistical Models for Research in Behavior Modification." *Journal of Experimental Education,* 1973, 41, pp. 54–63.

Kratchowill, T. R. (Ed.) *Single-Subject Research: Strategies for Evaluating Change.* New York: Academic Press, 1978.

Kratchowill, T., R. Mott, C. Dodson. "Case Study and Single-Case Research in Clinical and Applied Psychology." In A. Bellack and M. Hersen (Eds.). *Research Methods in Clinical Psychology,* New York: Pergamon Press, 1984.

Krishef, C. H. *Fundamental Statistics for Human Services and Social Work.* Boston: Duxbury Press, 1987.

Leitenburg, H. "The Use of Single-Case Methodology in Psychotherapy Research." *Journal of Abnormal Psychology,* 1973, 82:1, pp. 87–101.

Levy, Rona. "Overview of Single-Case Experiments." In A. Rosenblatt and D. Waldfogel (Eds.). *Handbook of Clinical Social Work.* Washington D.C.: Jossey-Bass, 1983.

Mann, R. A. "The Behavior-Therapeutic use of Contingency Contracting to Control an Adult Behavior Problem: Weight Control." *Journal of Applied Behavior Analysis,* 1972, 5, pp. 99–109.

Martin, J. and L. Epstein. "Evaluating Treatment Effectiveness in Cerebral Palsy: Single-Case Designs." *Physical Therapy,* 1976, 56, pp. 285–294.

McGeoch, J. A. and A. L. Irion. *The Psychology of Human Learning.* New York: Longmans, Green, 1952.

Parsonson, B. and D. Baer. "The Analysis and Presentation of Graphic Data." In T. Kratochwill (Ed.). *Single-Case Research: Strategies for Evaluating Change.* New York: Academic Press, 1978.

Prince, M. *The Dissociation of a Personality.* New York: Longmans, Green, 1905.

Rabin, C. "The Single-Case Design in Family Therapy Evaluation Research." *Family Process,* 1981, 20, pp. 351–366.

Revusky, S. H. "Some Statistical Treatments Compatible with Individual Organism Methodology." *Journal of the Experimental Analysis of Behavior,* 1967, 10, pp. 319–330.

Risley, T., and M. Wolf. "Strategies for Analyzing Behavioral Change Over Time," In *Lifespan Development Psychology: Methodological Issues.* Eds. N. Nesselroade and H. Reese. New York: Academic Press, 1972 pp. 175–183.

Scheffe, H. *The Analysis of Variance*. New York: Wiley, 1959.

Shewart, W. A. *Economic Control of Quality of Manufactured Products*. New York: Van Nostrand Reinhold, 1931.

Shine, L. C. and S. M. Bower. "A One-Way Analysis of Variance for Single-Subject Designs." *Educational and Psychological Measurement*, 1971, 31, pp. 105–113.

Shipley, T. (Ed.) *Classics in Psychology*. New York: Philosophical Library, 1961.

Sidman, M. *Tactics of Scientific Research: Evaluating Experimental Data in Psychology*. New York: Basic Books, 1960.

Skinner, B. F. "Operant Behavior," in W. K. Koing (Ed.) *Operant Behavior Areas of Research and Application*, New York: Appleton Century Crofts, 1966.

Stratton, G. M. "Vision Without Inversion of the Retinal Image," *Psychological Review*, 1897, 4, pp. 341–360, 463–481.

Strupp, H. and A. Bergin. "Some Empirical and Conceptual Bases for Coordinated Research in Psychotherapy: A Critical Review of Issues, Trends, and Evidence." *International Journal of Psychiatry*, 1969, 7, pp. 18–90.

Thomas, E. J. "Uses of Research Methods in Interpersonal Practice." In *Social Work Research* (Rev. ed.). Ed. N. A. Polansky. Chicago: University of Chicago Press: 1975, pp. 254–283.

Thomas, E. J. "Research and Service in Single-Case Experimentation: Conflicts and Choices." *Social Work Research and Abstracts*, 1978, 14, pp. 20–31.

Thoreson, C. "The Intensive Design: An Intimate Approach to Counseling Research." Paper read at American Educational Association, Chicago, 1972.

Toothaker, L. E., M. Banz, C. Noble, J. Camp, and D. Davis. "N = 1 Designs: The Failure of ANOVA-Based tests." *Journal of Educational Statistics*, 1983, 8, pp. 289–309.

Wampold, B. E. and N. L. Worsham. "Randomization Tests for Multiple Baseline Designs." *Behavioral Assessment*, 1986, 8, pp. 135–143.

Watson, J. B., and Rosalie Rayner. "Conditioned Emotional Reactions." *Journal of Experimental Psychology*, 1920, 3, pp. 1–14.

White, O. R. *A Manual for the Calculation and Use of the Median Slope—A Technique of Progress Estimation and Prediction in the Single Case*. Regional Resource Center for Handicapped Children, University of Oregon; Eugene, Oregon, 1972.

White, O. R. *The "Split Middle"—A "Quickie" Method of Trend Estimation*. Experimental Education Unit, Child Development and Mental Retardation Center, University of Washington, 1974.

AUTHOR INDEX

SUBJECT INDEX